MW01035250

Invisible Houston

Number Six: Texas A&M Southwestern Studies
ROBERT A. CALVERT *and* LARRY D. HILL
General Editors

Robert D. Bullard

Invisible Houston

THE BLACK EXPERIENCE IN BOOM AND BUST

TEXAS A&M UNIVERSITY PRESS : COLLEGE STATION

Frontispiece: Row houses, also known as "shotgun" houses, in
the Fourth Ward, 1983. (Photograph by Earlie Hudnall)

The paper used in this book meets the minimum requirements
of the American National Standard for Permanence
of Paper for Printed Library materials, Z39, 48–1984.
Building materials have been chosen for durability.

Library of Congress Cataloging-in-Publication Data

Bullard, Robert D. (Robert Doyle), 1946–
   Invisible Houston.
   (Texas A & M southwestern studies; no. 6)
   Bibliography: p.
   Includes index.
   1. Afro-Americans—Texas—Houston—Economic
conditions.   2. Afro-Americans—Texas—Houston—
Social conditions.   3. Houston (Tex.)—Economic
conditions.   4. Houston (Tex.)—Social conditions.
I. Title.   II. Series.
F394.H89N42 1987   305.8'96073'07641411   87–491
ISBN 0–89096–312–6
ISBN 0–89096–357–6 pbk.

To Nehemiah and Myrtle Bullard

Contents

Illustrations

TABLES

MAPS

Preface

This book grew out of my long-standing interest in the black experience and observations made as an urban sociologist at Texas Southern University in Houston. The idea for writing this book was in part sparked by the voluminous amount of material written on boomtown Houston in the mid-seventies and the dearth of published material on black Houston during this crucial period of the city's history. Much of the material that was produced during the seventies systematically omitted any discussion of the city's sizable black community. For the most part, institutional promoters of Boomtown treated the city's black community as an invisible community.

As a black person working in the midst of Houston's most diverse black neighborhood, the Third Ward, I did not take long to discover the interrelationship between institutional racism, poverty, illiteracy, unemployment, residential segregation, and crime and their impact on the lives of black community residents. In a sense, the Third Ward served as a microcosm of the larger black Houston community. This predominantly black neighborhood thus served as a social laboratory for a series of case studies that were conducted in the mid-seventies on black life in the urban ghetto. These studies were later expanded to include analyses of life in a number of other black Houston neighborhoods.

This book attempts to capture the broad institutional aspects of the black Houston community. It is by no means meant to be exhaustive of all aspects of black life in the city. However, my purpose is to provide the reader with a better understanding of the socio-historical and contemporary issues that affect black life in the nation's fourth largest city.

I am indebted to the National Science Foundation's Minority Research Initiation Program for sponsoring part of the research for this book under grant number RII–8413453. I would also like to thank a number of persons who assisted me in so many ways during the preparation of this book. Special thanks go to my colleague at Texas Southern University, L. Alex Swan, for his assistance and support within the Department of Sociology.

Special appreciation goes to Khosro Godazi for the highly commendable job performed on the graphics work, and to Betty McMurrin and Madelene Riggins, who were particularly diligent in typing the manuscript and its revisions.

I am profoundly grateful for the patience, understanding, and encouragement given me by Linda McKeever Bullard throughout this undertaking.

Invisible Houston

1.

Introduction:
Blacks and the New South

In the 1970s the southern United States underwent a transformation, changing from a "net exporter of people to a powerful human magnet." [1] The South thus became a major growth region in that decade. The expanding population, economic, and political bases spawned the notion that the Old South was rising up as the New South and that its cities were rising to claim their rightful place in the nation. A number of publications chronicled the changes which propelled the New South and numerous of its cities into the economic and political limelight. [2]

These changes, which continued to shape life-styles in the southern region in the 1980s, can be attributed to a number of factors. First, the South's climate became more attractive (especially to northerners, many of whom had found the heat and humidity of some southern cities to be unbearable) because of the widespread use of air conditioning, which allowed for more comfortable home and work environments. Second, the prevalence of right-to-work laws in southern states limited the presence of labor unions. The minimal presence of labor unions often meant a lower wage scale for workers in blue-collar and service occupations who had jobs similar to those of their higher-paid counterparts in the North. The lower prevailing wages in the South made the region attractive to cost-conscious industries looking for a place to relocate or expand. Third, the South had an abundance of open spaces and low population density areas near its major urban centers, and large parcels of this open, flat land could be purchased at very reasonable prices. Moreover, land-use controls and environmental regulations were less restrictive than in the North. Fourth, the political atmosphere was changed with the passage of the Voting Rights Act of 1965 and the subsequent redistricting plans that were based on population changes. The new political atmosphere was more representative of the region's population because the redistricting eventually enabled more blacks and Republicans to be elected from the newly created districts. Blacks and other ethnic minority group members intensified their struggle for political empowerment. Fifth, new opportunities in education, employment, and housing allowed southerners to make dramatic social gains. Finally, aggressive booster campaigns promoted southern cities as having a pro-business climate. Southern states fiercely recruited new businesses through special tax incentives, construction of new highways and access roads, publicly financed industrial parks for long-term lease by companies, the establishment of trade schools and junior colleges to train local workers, and other pro-business projects.[3]

There is no doubt that important gains have been made in the South since 1970. However, many enduring problems of the region have not been solved, and many have been ignored. This was true for the "boom" period of the seventies and the "bust" period of the early and mid-eighties. Uneven development within the region has intensified the social and economic inequalities between blacks and whites. Those newcomers and native southerners who had marginal skills generally found themselves in the region's growing unemployment lines. The individuals who did not have the requisite education and skills often became part of an emerging urban underclass in the South. Poverty existed alongside the new affluence. Moreover, this poverty was essential; it represented the large pool of cheap, nonunionized labor that was part of the region's so-called "good business climate."[4]

The problem of institutional racism has continued to permeate nearly every institution in the region, and it has caused serious problems for many of the New South's longtime residents, namely, its black community. For the purposes of this book, the black community is "a highly diversified set of interrelated structures and aggregates of people who are held together by the forces of white oppression and racism."[5] In the boom of the Sunbelt, very little has been done to address the problem of deteriorating infrastructures within the black community, and many southern cities have found themselves in a pattern similar to that of their northern counterparts. A dwindling tax base, inadequate public services, loss of low- and moderate-priced housing stock, strained employment markets, rising crime rates, drug trafficking, business closures and disinvestment, and a host of other urban ills severely threaten the stability of many black communities in the South.

The South has always been home to a large share of the nation's blacks. More than 90 percent of black Americans lived in the southern United States at the turn of the century. A little more than one-half (53 percent) of the nation's blacks were living in the South in 1980, the same percentage as in 1970.[6] Until the mid-seventies the South had seen more blacks leave the region than migrate to it. However, between 1975 and 1980 more than 415,000 blacks moved to the South, while 220,000 left the region (a net in-migration of 195,000 blacks). More than 411,000 blacks migrated to the South between 1980 and 1985, while 324,000 moved out of the region (a net in-migration of 87,000 blacks). These figures clearly point to a "reversal of the longstanding black exodus."[7]

Within the South blacks made up a sizable share of the population. In 1980 they were one-fifth of the population in the twelve southern states of the Old Confederacy, and there were 14 million blacks in the greater South Region (18.6 percent of the population).[8] Blacks made up 9.9 percent of the Northeast Region, 9.1 percent of the North Central Region, and only 5.2 percent of the West Region.

The black population in the South is concentrated in the major urban centers of the region. Southern cities of 100,000 or more attracted the bulk of blacks who migrated to the region. These large cities also attracted the lion's share of black rural-to-urban and urban-to-urban migration within the southern states.

The challenge that many of the South's major cities must face is resource allocation. How will the region's jobs, housing, public services, political representation, and overall benefits and burdens be shared with its racial and ethnic minority groups? Blacks have a long history of unequal treatment in the Deep South, and many poverty pockets remain. During the Sunbelt expansion era, the tendency was to build new factories where there was surplus white labor and to avoid places with high concentrations of poor and unskilled blacks. The fact that blacks were deemed more likely than whites to join labor unions was a major factor in some industry relocation decisions.[9] As agriculture became mechanized and even nonagricultural opportunities decreased in the rural South, many blacks migrated to the region's big cities, thereby swelling the already growing southern ghettos. Black residents of the southern ghettos were thus racially and economically segregated from expanding job opportunities and new industries.

The urban ghettos and rural poverty pockets in the South have been as difficult to eliminate as the slums in the Northeast and Midwest. Many southern cities are firmly on the path toward social and fiscal problems similar to those experienced by cities in other parts of the country. Southern cities now attract more low-income migrants than they lose. These cities face "increasing difficulties in providing community services to their sprawling low-income neighborhoods." [10]

Chet Fuller, a black journalist, traveled across the South and discovered that the "much touted progress of some southern cities is more illusion than reality." [11] Although the New South has been portrayed as booming with industrial growth and employment opportunities that were once closed to blacks, and although there has been progress for some southern blacks, very little has changed for the majority of blacks. Fuller summed up his observations on the power arrangement and economic structure in the South: "Power has not changed hands in the South, not from white hands to black hands. Economics is the great controller. Economics is money is power is still white. Until we realize that and move to cooperate more fully with one another to take greater control of our economic destiny, there will be no New South." [12]

The New South has, unfortunately, meant business as usual for millions of blacks. As blacks increasingly migrated to large southern cities in search of the new opportunities, these areas, which already had high concentrations of poor blacks, became growing ghettos and pockets of poverty. This occurred even as the region was experiencing a parallel boom in employment and housing. Institutional barriers continue to deny an equitable share of the region's wealth to a significant portion of the South's population. This was the pattern in the Old South, and the conditions that gave rise to the New South have not eliminated it.

Although many of the overt manifestations of racial discrimination no longer exist in the South, more subtle and sophisticated forms of denial have been used to produce similar results. The grim reality of conditions for many blacks in large southern cities was ignored by the pointed promotional campaigns that were designed to attract new businesses to the region, but they were also used to change the stereotypical image of the South as a socially and economically backward region. The message that the South had joined the twentieth century and the rest of the country came across loud and clear. The national media singled out several showcase cities for their progress in the social, economic, and political arenas. For example, Atlanta became known as the "capital" of the New South primarily because of its commercial dominance, which included a high concentration of Fortune 500 businesses, as well as many government offices and administrative headquarters. The city be-came the transportation hub of the South. Atlanta also became well known for its progressive political leadership and race relations. It was promoted as a "city too busy to hate."

Houston soon emerged as the premier Sunbelt city in the mid-1970s, becoming the mecca of thousands of individuals seeking new op-portunities. More than five thousand persons each month migrated to "Boomtown USA" during the city's heyday, the mid-seventies. The rela-tively low cost of living, the large number of new jobs created, the phe-nomenal growth in housing units, combined with the potential for earn-ing an above-average income all contributed to Houston's being tagged the "golden buckle" of the Sunbelt.[13]

Houston's population had increased to nearly 1.6 million persons in 1980, making it the nation's fifth largest city. By 1982, Houston had re-placed Philadelphia as the nation's fourth largest city. Although there was a great deal of attention focused on the city's phenomenal growth, the area's racial and ethnic diversity received somewhat superficial cov-erage. This glossing over was especially typical of Houston's institu-tional promoters, who consistently treated the city's ethnic diversity as a point best served by omission. The end result of Houston's image-management campaigns was the minority (black and Hispanic) commu-nity's status as an "invisible" community. This was not a small point when one considers the fact that blacks and Hispanics made up more than 45 percent of Houston's population in 1980.[14]

Upon my arrival in Houston and at Texas Southern University in the summer of 1976, I was somewhat overwhelmed by the massive coverage by both the local and national media of the Houston "success" story. The booster campaigns of Houston promoters were at first highly con-vincing to an outsider like me. Yet the constant headlining in daily news-papers and on television gradually undermined its own message and created the impression that Houston was a city struggling to build an image. Over the years Houston had affectionately been tagged the "Mag-nolia City," "Bayou City," "Space City," and "Boomtown" by city pro-motional campaigns,[15] and in 1984 the city initiated yet another image-building campaign, "Houston Proud," under the leadership of the Houston Chamber of Commerce. Whereas the booster campaigns of the 1970s saw Houston take the offense (boasting a strong economy and growing population), the Houston Proud campaign of the 1980s was largely defensive in nature.

Houston Proud and similar ad campaigns in the eighties were designed specifically to counteract the negative publicity which has surrounded the city's faltering economy. Hard economic times befell Boomtown in the eighties because of the city's heavy dependence on the oil and petrochemical industry, hard hit by the worldwide oil glut and plunging price of oil. Although the impetus for the promotional messages changed from the 1970s to the 1980s, the treatment of the city's black community by Chamber of Commerce publications, local newspapers, and public school districts' and local college and university publicity during both eras did not. Black faces were rarely seen in material which promoted or defended the city's image. Houston's black community remained invisible to the city's image builders.

The black media have also participated in the diffusion of information in their rating of Houston as one of the best cities for blacks during the seventies. The rating schemes of many black publications have gone beyond mere promotional campaigns. For example, black magazines such as *Ebony, Essence,* and *Black Enterprise* have used demographic (size of the black population), social (civil rights), economic (size of the black middle class, income, unemployment, education, home ownership, and business ownership), and political (blacks in elected and appointed offices) factors in their rating of the best cities for blacks. Although the rating schemes have provided some useful information on the conditions of blacks in major cities across the country, they do have their drawbacks. Comparisons were usually made between blacks in one city and blacks in another city. This is equivalent to comparing apples with oranges. Such comparisons ignore the disparities that often exist between blacks and whites. A rating scheme which focuses on black-white income comparisons in Houston, for example, covers an altogether different dimension than income comparisons which focus on blacks in Houston and blacks in Atlanta.

An even more puzzling element of the Houston image issue involved the dearth of popular as well as scholarly material on the city's diverse black community. Despite that lack, though, it was not difficult for me to discover the city within the city—black Houston—and its rich, contrasting imagery. My third-floor office at Texas Southern University provided a picturesque view of Houston's most diverse black neighborhood, the Third Ward, a microcosm of the city's larger black community.[16] From my office I was able to observe in the foreground one of the city's oldest public housing projects built for blacks (Cuney Homes), rows of "shotgun" houses, well-maintained single-family brick homes, black churches sprinkled throughout the area, storefront shops and small business establishments, and a host of daily interactions which make up the urban black experience. The background of these black community institutions was the towering and sparkling Houston skyline.

The disparities between black and white Houston existed in both the boom of the 1970s and the bust of the 1980s. The city's black economic underclass constitutes a sizable share of the city's population. The poverty level for Houston as a whole stood at 12.7 percent in 1980 but was over 22 percent for the city's blacks.[17] Median family income for black Houstonians was $15,442, compared with $25,669 for white Houstonians.[18] The city's blacks earned only 60 percent of the income earned by whites. The income gap of more than $10,000 that separated these two groups in 1980 in all likelihood widened with the economic recession that began in 1982.

The Houston-area unemployment rate remained low throughout the decade of the seventies. For instance, unemployment in the Houston Standard Metropolitan Statistical Area (SMSA) averaged 4.0 percent in 1975, 3.3 percent in 1979, and 4.2 percent in 1980. The unemployment rate for blacks was double that for whites during this period. Unemployment in the Houston metropolitan area began an upward spiral early in the eighties. The January, 1981, unemployment rate was 4.6 percent overall, 3.8 percent for whites, and nearly twice that rate—7.5 percent—for blacks. The area's unemployment rate jumped from 4.6 percent in January, 1981, to 9.1 percent in January of 1983.[19] For the same period, black unemployment increased from 7.5 percent to 15.2 percent. The unemployment gap between blacks and whites actually widened after the 1982 recession. The black unemployment rate was 2.9 percentage points higher than the white unemployment rate in January 1982, but was 6.1 percentage points higher a year later. Blacks were 17.2 percent of the Houston area work force but constituted more than 28.7 percent of the unemployed workers. The unemployment gap remained high throughout the bust period of the mid-eighties. The January, 1986, unemployment rate was 5.7 percent for whites and 12.5 percent for blacks, a difference of nearly 7 percentage points.[20]

Black workers have had difficulty not only in getting employment but also in keeping their jobs. Black Houstonians were less likely than whites to be employed in the city's boomtown economy. They were more likely to be laid off during economic hard times. Black workers often lack seniority or tenure, thus making them especially vulnerable in layoff plans.[21] The distribution of black workers in the labor market also contributed to this group's making up a larger share of the unemployed.

The 1980 figures reveal that black workers were less likely than white workers to be employed in white-collar occupations (occupations which generally have lower unemployment rates). Only 39.1 percent of blacks in the Houston area were employed in white-collar occupations as compared with 64.2 percent of the whites. More than 40 percent of blacks and 28 percent of whites were employed in blue-collar occupations in 1980.[22]

Depressionlike conditions in a host of Houston's older black neighborhoods did not magically appear overnight. Many of the city's ghetto residents were impoverished, inadequately housed, shortchanged by inner-city schools, discriminated against, victimized by criminals, dehumanized by the criminal justice system, and politically powerless during the height of the city's growth period of 1970 to 1980. The prevailing sentiment has been "out of sight, out of mind." Although some gains have been made, institutional barriers have restricted the upward mobility of blacks and trapped many of them in an unending cycle of poverty.

Institutionalized racism continues to define the existence of thousands of black Houstonians in employment, education, home and business ownership, health care, the judicial system, the social welfare structure, politics, and the spatial environment. Houston has developed a growth pattern that is economically and racially segmented. More than 81 percent of Houston's blacks lived in mostly black neighborhoods in 1980 as compared with 93 percent in 1970 and 1960, 91 percent in 1950, and 84 percent in 1940.[23]

Blacks, Hispanics, and whites are clustered in different sectors of the city. These sectors are worlds apart and are defined by class. Black and white communities are separate, and unequal. The residents of these disparate worlds seldom see each other, much less each other's worlds.[24] The only contact these groups may have is on the job. Thus, economics is the only link between these groups; government policies have been the "proximate and essential cause of urban apartheid." [25] Apartheid-type housing policies have contributed to the separation of blacks and other visible ethnic minorities from whites and the poor from the affluent.

The sociospatial groupings that have emerged in Houston are a result of the distribution of wealth, patterns of racial and economic discrimination, access to jobs and housing, real-estate practices, and a host of other sociological factors. Conversely, the ability to escape an unfavorable physical environment is roughly proportional to affluence. It is much easier for a family to escape poor housing, high crime, and pollution if that family has money. Limited financial resources and institutional barriers, a kind of double jeopardy, relegate many black Houstonians to lower-quality residential areas (as measured in terms of housing quality, residential amenities, accessibility of employment and shopping centers, air and water quality, and municipal services).

Houston's expansionist strategy in the 1970s—aggressive annexation of outlying areas—did add to the tax base, but often at the expense of older inner-city neighborhoods. The city's burgeoning growth "made the inequities between its vital, well-maintained neighborhoods and those falling or fallen into decay all the more apparent."[26] City services in older minority neighborhoods suffered severely as a direct result of the city's attempt to provide services to newly annexed areas, which were mostly white. There were black areas, Riceville and Bordersville, that were annexed in the late sixties and still waiting to receive city services as late as 1981. These two Houston neighborhoods have been surrounded by commercial and residential development, and their residents are invisible.

To understand fully how blacks and their neighborhoods have remained invisible, one must understand the impact of racism on the institutions in which this image is created. White racism "systematically provides economic, political, psychological, and social advantages for whites at the expense of blacks and other people of color."[27] In promotional and news release material distributed by the city, black leaders, landmarks, and institutions are nowhere to be found. For instance, it is not uncommon to find promotional maps of Houston that show the location of the mostly white University of Houston but not Texas Southern University (TSU), which is mostly black. These two state universities are adjacent to each other, separated only by Scott Street, but the one on the wrong side of that unofficial line of demarcation is invisible.

Texas Southern University was established in 1947 by the Texas legislature, which was desperately attempting to keep blacks out of the University of Texas School of Law and to short-circuit an impending lawsuit by the National Association for the Advancement of Colored People (NAACP).[28] The U.S. Supreme Court, in the famous 1950 *Sweatt* v. *Painter* decision, finally compelled the University of Texas and similar schools to admit blacks to their graduate and professional schools. It is ironic that white racism created Texas State University for Negroes, as TSU was originally named, and has perpetuated its invisibility and second-class status.

The discriminatory practices built into the education, housing, employment, and legal environment and the institutions of the black community show that there is a city buried within the larger Houston community. This book attempts to describe in broad terms black Houston, beginning with its meager origin in Freedmen's Town shortly after emancipation in Texas on June 19, 1865—"Juneteenth"—and proceeding through the first half of the 1980s. Although the black experience during the pre-1970 era (the Great Depression years, the struggles of the forties and fifties, and the civil rights movement of the sixties) is covered, the major focus of the analysis is on the "boom-and-bust" era of the 1970s and 1980s. Many structural aspects of the black experience have been slow to change and in some cases, conditions have actually worsened. An analysis of the black experience in Houston is thus a study of struggle and inequality regardless of era or focus. The boom-bust economic cycle, however, may have little relevance for explaining the conditions of individuals who have been locked into poverty and form a permanent underclass. This underclass existed in prosperous times and hard economic times.

In an effort to provide insights into the black experience in Houston, I have presented the discussion in nine succeeding chapters. Chapter 2 traces the early beginning of the city's black community to its present status as the largest black community in the southern United States. Chapter 3 analyzes residential patterns, home ownership trends, and neighborhood transition during the city's "boomtown" era (1970–80). The issues in housing the poor are presented in chapter 4. The major areas covered there include government commitment and public support for subsidized housing, the politics of public housing, and the controversy surrounding site selection criteria for low- and moderate-income housing. Chapter 5 looks at the persisting problem of housing discrimination and barriers to decent housing for blacks and other minorities, and for families with children. Government legislation, namely, the Federal Fair Housing Act of 1968 and Houston's Fair Housing Ordinance of 1975, is reviewed to determine the extent to which such laws have been effective in providing open housing for blacks.

Chapter 6 focuses on issues of pollution and quality of life in the black community and in Houston as a whole. Specifically, the section explores environmental quality concerns within Houston neighborhoods, the impact of the city's no-zoning policy on land use, the efficacy of deed restrictions in protecting residential areas, and civic leaders' evaluation of government and industry response to the city's pollution problem. The chapter also presents data which demonstrate the inequitable distribution of waste disposal facilities in the city.

Chapter 7 is a discussion of income, employment, and educational trends of black Houston in comparison with the larger community during the seventies and early eighties. Included in this section is an analysis of poverty, the growing underclass, and the mismatch between workers' skills and the changing job market. Black business and economic development trends in Houston and other major cities are analyzed in chapter 8. Comparative data on size, type, and gross receipts of Houston's black-owned businesses are analyzed for 1977 and 1982.

Chapter 9 concentrates on crime, law enforcement, manpower needs, police-community relations, and policing in the black community. The final chapter analyzes the city's changing black leadership, civil rights and equity issues, the continuing battle over school desegregation, and black political gains made after the passage of the Voting Rights Act of 1965.

It is my hope that these insights into the Houston experience from a black perspective will facilitate the discovery of the rich cultural life present in Houston's black community and thus reduce its invisibility. Moreover, I am hopeful that this book will awaken the South's largest black community to realize its economic and political potential and to take a more active role in the future growth and development of the city.

2.

The South's Largest
Black Community

For much of its history, Houston was considered a boomtown in the Southwest. The city was founded in 1836 just six months after Sam Houston's victory over the Mexican army at San Jacinto. The two New York businessmen who began it, Augustus and John Kirby Allen, were certain that the newly independent Republic of Texas would attract a steady stream of settlers to the area, and they proved to be quite correct. Kenneth Wheeler, in his study of urban growth in Texas, described the early Houston era: "Houston boomed to the extent that it was soon considered the grand focus of the Republic. It was a raw and explosive town where economic competition was ruthless, yet community cooperation was notable."[1]

The site on which Houston was founded was not the most habitable location. The swampy, subtropical setting was a challenge to the early developers, who had the original town site cleared by black slaves and Mexican laborers because, believed the entrepreneurs, "no white man could have worked and endured the insect bites and malaria, snake bites, impure water, and other hardships." Later on, black slaves in Houston were primarily domestic servants or worked on the wharves and in the trades.[2]

The black population in Houston remained relatively small until after the Civil War. On Emancipation Day in Texas there were approximately one thousand blacks in Houston, but after Juneteenth, newly freed blacks began moving to the city to seek opportunities. Thousands of freed blacks migrated from the cotton-rich Brazos River bottomlands to found "Freedmen's Town," which was part of Houston's Fourth Ward, about 1866. Don E. Carleton and Thomas H. Kreneck, in their history of early Houston, point out that "an influx of black migrants to Houston filled the growing demand for labor. . . . As their numbers increased, blacks developed their own separate society, centering primarily around their Methodist and Baptist churches." [3]

Freedmen's Town became a thriving center of black business and commerce as well as black cultural and social life; more than 95 percent of Houston's black-owned businesses were in the Fourth Ward. [4] West Dallas Street became the heart of Houston's black business district. This neighborhood had its own community facility, Pilgrim Temple, which provided office space for Houston's black professionals, their social and cultural events, and the office of the Houston Citizens Chamber of Commerce (called the Negro Chamber of Commerce when it was founded in 1935). That famous black landmark was demolished in the sixties to make way for the construction of Interstate 45 and elevated streets.

Gladys House, an active member of the Freedmen's Town Association (a nonprofit organization dedicated to preserving the Fourth Ward/ Freedmen's Town neighborhood), summarized the historical significance of that neighborhood to Houston's black community:

> Houston's finest black professionals were products of Freedmen's Town. . . . Today's Allen Parkway Village [a public housing project] covers the original site of Freedmen's Town. The construction of Allen Parkway Village caused displacement of many black property owners and black professionals. Yet, its completion in 1949 discriminated against blacks.
> Black businesses flourished up to Travis Street, north to Franklin Street, south to Bell, and west to Taft. But this was to last only until the 30's and 40's. The city's downtown area began to expand. City Hall, the Coliseum, and Sam Houston Park replaced residential and business structures of the black community. [5]

Black settlers of Freedmen's Town, former slaves and their descendants, had acquired ownership of most of the land in the community by the 1880s; this amazing feat was accomplished by a poor and illiterate group less than one generation removed from slavery. But blacks began to lose ownership of the land in the neighborhood during the 1920s, and the Great Depression years of the thirties saw an ongoing erosion of black landownership in the Fourth Ward. This process has continued to the present. Although this dilapidated neighborhood has experienced gradual physical and economic decline over the years, the land on which it stands is some of the most valuable real estate in Houston. [6]

The inhabitants of Houston's Fourth Ward in 1980 were primarily renters (less than 5 percent of the housing in the neighborhood was owner-occupied)—elderly, black, and poor. In addition, as Gladys

Above: Former slaves residing in Harris County, 1915 (photograph courtesy of the Houston Metropolitan Research Center, Houston Public Library). *Below:* Rev. Jack Yates, late 1800s (photograph courtesy of Mrs. Olee Yates McCullough).

Above: Antioch Missionary Baptist Church (founded in 1866), 1984 (photograph by R. D. Bullard). *Below:* Emancipation Park, in the Third Ward, 1984 (photograph by Earlie Hudnall).

House noted, the neighborhood lies in the path of westward expansion of Houston's central business district. These demographic factors make the Fourth Ward neighborhood a prime area for wholesale displacement of its residents.[7]

Although few blacks owned land in the Fourth Ward in the 1980s, a legacy of the neighborhood lives on in its churches. This neighborhood of some sixty-eight hundred residents has more than twenty churches. The most notable is Antioch Baptist Church. Listed on the National Register of Historic Places, it is the oldest black church in Texas, dating back to the mid-1860s.[8] The church's first full-time pastor, Rev. Jack Yates, was a well-known and respected black leader in Texas. Jack Yates Senior High School, located in the Third Ward, bears his name. Antioch Baptist Church and another black church, Trinity Methodist Church, were instrumental in the purchase of land in 1872 for Emancipation Park to commemorate the freeing of slaves in Texas. That park remains a cultural landmark in Houston's black community.

BOOSTERISM AND THE GROWTH OF BLACK HOUSTON

One of the early boosters of Houston as a city of opportunity for blacks was the *Informer,* a weekly newspaper. The newspaper maintained an aggressive posture in selling blacks on Houston, underscoring the idea that blacks could expect "unexcelled industrial opportunities" in the city, which was affectionately called "Heavenly Houston."[9] And even though the growing black population intensified the prejudices of whites, resulting in the enforcement of Jim Crow laws to control blacks and to institutionalize racial discrimination, "Heavenly Houston" continued to attract black migrants. Houston's black workers were restricted primarily to traditional, low-wage "Negro" jobs as cooks, custodians, and domestics, and racism permeated every social and economic institution in the city, including housing, education, and employment.

Residential segregation became the dominant housing pattern in the Bayou City. Racially identifiable neighborhoods became more pronounced between 1875 and 1930, when "there were two separate societies [black and white] connected only by economic necessity." A 1929 Houston City Planning Commission report strongly endorsed complete separation of the races. In essence, the report stated that "because of long established racial prejudices, it is best for both races that living areas be segregated."[10]

A number of Houston's older black suburban enclaves have been encircled by a sea of whiteness. Black neighborhoods that were once located on Houston's urban fringe and were semi-rural in character are now surrounded by new commercial development and subdivisions. Many of the residents of these older black suburbs have been untouched by the new wave of building and development in their areas. Houston's Riceville and Bordersville are classic examples of systematic neglect and the deliberate exclusion of progress from these areas.

Riceville, an all-black neighborhood, is located in southwest Houston. Founded by Leonard Rice, the neighborhood dates back to the 1850s, when it was developed as an insular, rural farm community. The present Riceville is principally located near South Gessner, South Braeswood, and West Bellfort streets. It had its own school located on South Gessner (the street's name was changed from Riceville School Road) between West Bellfort and South Braeswood. The Old Riceville School, later renamed Braes Bayou Elementary School, was an all-black, segregated school operated by Harris County until 1913; the Houston Independent School District acquired the school and operated it from 1914 until 1967. Thus Braes Bayou Elementary School operated under both Harris County and HISD as an all-black school. The school typified the systematic neglect and disparate treatment accorded the Riceville community prior to and after the area's annexation by the City of Houston. Because of increased pressure from the federal courts to dismantle the dual public school system and the overt disparities between black and white schools, Brays Bayou Elementary was condemned in 1967. The Riceville children were transferred to schools in the Sunnyside neighborhood. The Sunnyside neighborhood schools were also mostly black.

Although the annexation by the city occurred in the sixties, Riceville still did not have many city services as late as 1982. Public water facilities did not serve the Riceville area, city sanitary sewers were not provided, and storm drainage and runoff water flowed along roadside ditches to open drainage ditches. Even now, the streets in the neighborhood are gravel-topped roads riddled with potholes.[11]

Change was slow to come to the Riceville community. For the most part, Riceville Mount Olive Baptist Church, founded in 1889 by the Reverend John Lilly, is still the hub of the sparsely populated community. The original site of the church was north of Keegans Bayou on White Chapel Road. However, key demographic changes in this community and the surrounding area can be traced to the mid-fifties, when

Above: Houston Colored High School, 1914 (photograph courtesy of the Houston Metropolitan Research Center, Houston Public Library). *Below:* Houston Colored Carnegie Library, 1926 (photograph courtesy of the Houston Metropolitan Research Center, Houston Public Library).

subdivisions were developed nearby for whites. Blacks were excluded from these new subdivisions by deed restrictions or the whites-only marketing and sales policies of realtors. White subdivision development accelerated during the sixties, and black landownership in the area began to decline. By the mid-sixties, the Riceville Mount Olive Baptist Church and its cemetery had been surrounded by development and cut off from the portion of the Riceville community that survived. Vandalism became an increasing problem at the church, appearing to coincide with the rapid buildup of white neighborhoods across Keegans Bayou. The church was plagued by broken windows, and gravestones in the church's cemetery were moved on several occasions. A fire of suspicious origin destroyed the old church in the late sixties, and the congregation moved to a new site in Riceville. The Riceville Mount Olive Baptist Church was rebuilt in 1971 at its present location on South Gessner near West Bellfort.[12]

The Riceville community is currently surrounded by commercial buildings and expensive homes. One may stand on any Riceville street and see the $100,000 and $200,000 houses and buildings that have been constructed on the far side of the fence that separates the old neighborhood from the more recent settlers. The Riceville neighborhood has dwindled to less than three hundred inhabitants. Most of the housing in the area, much of it built between 1940 and 1954, is deteriorating. The future of the neighborhood is uncertain; many of the younger residents have left the area.

Although the problems that confront this black suburban neighborhood are many, there remains a strong sense of community. Black property owners in the Riceville community have come to realize that their neighborhood is strategically located in this busy section of southwest Houston. Many residents have taken the position that they will not sell their land.

Nearly thirty miles north of the Riceville community is another all-black suburban neighborhood with similar problems—Bordersville. Bordersville is an old sawmill settlement that was annexed by Houston in the mid-sixties as part of a corridor to the new Houston Intercontinental Airport. Ginger Hester described a Bordersville household's situation:

> This black community on the fringes of FM 1960 and suburbia is catching up with the 20th century. Jessie Doyle heads a household teaming with children; four are her daughter's, one is her brother's, one youngster is her own. Almost 10 people share the three-room shack, built in the late 1920s, like simi-

lar shanties along the dirt and gravel road, to house workers at Edgar Bor-
ders' now-defunct sawmill. Like the rest of the "sawmill quarters," it barely
hangs together with scraps of tar paper and rotting wood. The front door is
broken, without a working latch or lock, and also in need of repair is a
broken window pane, allowing cold air to blow in next to a small wood-
burning stove. She pays $10 a month rent and subtracts from that any repair
costs, and repairs are not high on the priority list.[13]

The problems of this neighborhood are similar to those in Riceville:
the lack of running water, sewer lines, paved streets, regular street repairs, and other neighborhood amenities that many Houstonians take for
granted. Some of the two hundred houses in the neighborhood have in-
door plumbing—mostly those houses that were built later. Until recently, most of the residents in the neighborhood had to get their water
from a "yellow city tank truck that makes door-to-door deliveries three
times a week, charging $2.98 per month for all the water delivered."[14]
In 1981 Bordersville became part of Houston's Community Development
Block Grant program, a federally funded program designed to assist
lower-income neighborhoods in making capital improvements, upgrading housing, and promoting economic development to create jobs. As a
neighborhood target area, Bordersville was earmarked to receive funds
to improve services in the area, and city hall spent some $500,000 on
new water lines for the area. But many of the residents could not benefit
from the new water lines because of the poor condition of their houses.
The city requires that homes meet the housing code before they can receive a hook-up, but most residents cannot afford the repairs needed to
meet the minimum standard, and city council policy limits the amount
of federal funds that can be spent on individual residences. In a situation that sings of Catch-22, some Bordersville residents continued to go
without.

The Bordersville Neighborhood Council has been an active group in
raising funds to assist residents, many of whom are elderly as well as
being poor, to pay for the water connection fees, which range from six
hundred to eight hundred dollars per household. The pressure of potential commercial or residential development will come to bear on this
suburban neighborhood because it straddles the affluent FM 1960 area
and is within close sight of U.S. Highway 59.

Bordersville remains a pocket of poverty amid the bustling area near
Houston Intercontinental Airport. The rapid development of the area
surrounding the airport overshadowed the conditions that exist for
nearby Bordersville residents. Moreover, the future of this neighbor-

hood is clouded by the fact that few of the residents have clear title to the property to which they have fallen heir, and court litigation over title disputes will likely increase with any new development in the area.

The concept of unrestrained capitalism that caused Houston to expand and envelop these black enclaves served as a magnet that attracted people from throughout the country and the world. Houston's population had grown from a mere 2,396 in 1850 to more than 44,633 in 1900.[15] While the city's overall size increased, its black population also expanded during this fifty-year period. There were more than 14,608 blacks in Houston (32.7 percent of the city's population) by 1900. Yet through the first half of the twentieth century black population growth began to decline in proportion to the city's expanding white population. It was not until 1960 that the percentage of blacks in the Houston population again showed an increase (Table 2.1).[16]

Houston's city limits expanded from a mere 9 square miles in 1850 to more than 550 square miles in 1980. The black population is located in a broad belt that extends from the south-central and southeast portions of the city into the northeast and north-central areas. Houston's black population has remained residentially segregated from the larger group during the past thirty years. Henry A. Bullock, a noted black sociologist, described the concentration of Houston's blacks in the 1950s: "Houston's Negro population is very tightly concentrated in a few areas. Although the population has responded to the suburban movement like all other urban populations, tradition has prevented basic changes in the geography of Negro settlement."[17]

Table 2.1. City of Houston Total Black Population, 1900–1980.

Year	Total Population	Black Population	Percent Black
1900	44,633	14,608	32.7
1910	78,800	23,929	30.4
1920	138,276	33,960	24.6
1930	292,352	63,337	21.7
1940	384,514	86,302	21.4
1950	596,163	125,400	21.0
1960	938,219	215,037	22.9
1970	1,232,802	316,552	25.7
1980	1,595,138	440,346	27.6

Source: U.S. Bureau of the Census, *Census of Population and Housing 1900, 1910, 1920, 1930, 1940, 1950, 1960, 1970, 1980.*

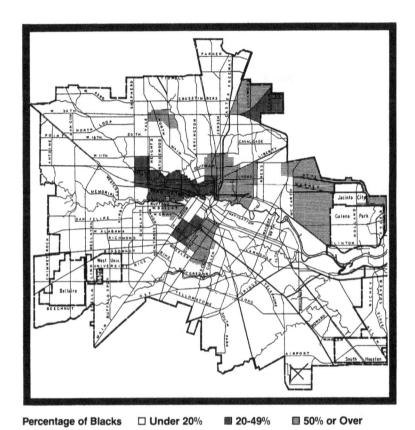

Percentage of Blacks   □ Under 20%   ▦ 20-49%   ▨ 50% or Over

Map 2.1. Black population in Houston, 1950. Based on map 1, "Geographic Distribution of the Houston Negro Population According to Percent Composing Each Census Tract, 1950," in Henry A. Bullock, *Pathways to the Houston Negro Market,* p. 63.

Map 2.1 shows the concentration of black Houston residents in 1950. Approximately two-thirds of the city's black population was concentrated in three major neighborhoods. The Fifth Ward, in northeast Houston, was the largest black area, with more than 40,680 inhabitants in 1950; the Third Ward, located in south-central Houston, had more than 29,168 blacks; and the Fourth Ward was home to more than 9,051 blacks in 1950 (Map 2.1).

Bullock described the pressures on the Fourth and Third Wards: "The Fourth Ward has long been associated with Houston's Negro life. Its immediate proximity to the downtown district exposes this area to the impact of urban territorial expansion first. Therefore, the area is highly transitional, and many of its families are seeking dwelling accommodations elsewhere. . . . However, the [Third Ward] is rapidly expanding to include adjacent tracts. The expansion is a result of increased population pressure from the Fourth Ward area, but is occasioned by the successful infiltration of Negro families into the white areas adjacent to Third Ward." [18]

Beginning in the fifties and accelerating in the sixties and seventies, the city's black population expanded outward, away from the central

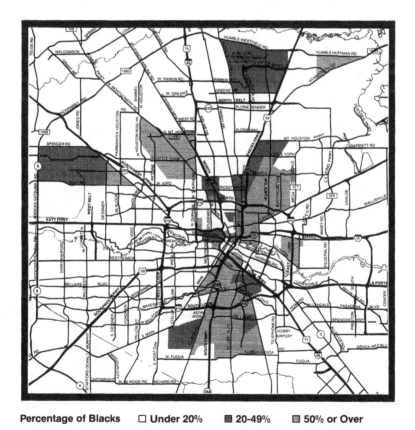

Percentage of Blacks   □ Under 20%   ▦ 20-49%   ▤ 50% or Over

Map 2.2. Black population in Houston–Harris County, 1970. (Base map by Key Maps, Inc., lic. no. 93.)

Percentage of Blacks   □ **Under 20%**   ▣ **20-49%**   ▤ **50% or Over**

Map 2.3. Black population in Houston–Harris County, 1980. (Base map by Key Maps, Inc., lic. no. 93.)

city, but it continued to be concentrated in these outlying areas, generally in the northeast and southeast quadrants of the city. Houston's black population was largely concentrated in census tracts on the eastern side of the city in 1970 and 1980 (see Maps 2.2 and 2.3). A comparison of the 1970 and 1980 maps shows how the boundaries of Houston's traditional black neighborhoods have been extended. The black population is indeed becoming more decentralized (that is, located away from the central business district), but residential segregation continues to be the controlling factor in the pattern of location of Houston's black residents.[19]

THE RISE AND FALL OF THE THIRD AND THE FIFTH

Like the Fourth Ward, the Third and the Fifth both have rich histories as black areas. Just as West Dallas Street was closely associated with the Fourth Ward, Dowling Street and Lyons Avenue were associated with the Third Ward and the Fifth Ward, respectively. These two neighborhoods emerged as predominantly black areas amidst the demands and pressures that existed after World War II. During this period there was increased demand for housing, and whites began to move out of the Fourth and Fifth Ward areas. Blacks were attached to these areas, however, because they offered home ownership opportunities for veterans as well as the growing number of other blacks who could afford to buy. Also, at that time, Fifth Ward was one of the few areas of Houston where blacks were permitted to own homes and operate businesses. In the 1960s blacks began to move southward from the Third Ward and northward from the Fifth Ward; the concentration of the city's black population along these corridors (northeast and southeast) still existed in the mid-1980s.

Strong competition and rivalries, probably most pronounced in athletic competitions, developed among the various black neighborhoods. The athletic rivalry between Phyllis Wheatley High School, in Fifth Ward, and Jack Yates High School, in Third Ward, epitomized this competition. The competition between those two schools represented more than a sports event or game and held the emotions of the entire Houston black community.

The Fifth Ward is the neighborhood lying just north of Houston's central business district. The boundaries of Fifth Ward include Buffalo Bayou on the south, Lockwood Drive on the west, Lorraine and the Southern Pacific Railroad on the north, and Elysian Street on the east. The development of the area dates back to the early 1860s. By the onset of World War II, it was predominantly black, and by 1950 it was Houston's most heavily populated black area.[20]

The census tracts that make up the neighborhood experienced a steady decline in population during the 1970s, and the 1980 population of the area was less than one-half what it had been in 1950. Still, more than 90 percent of the residents in Fifth Ward are black. The Fifth Ward neighborhood consists largely of single-family residences, along with some nonresidential land uses. For example, industry is concentrated on the southern boundary.[21]

Above: Houston Negro Hospital, later renamed Riverside General Hospital, 1926 (photograph courtesy of the Houston Metropolitan Research Center, Houston Public Library). *Below:* Barbara Jordan, first black elected to the Texas Senate and former member of the U.S. House of Representatives (photograph by Earlie Hudnall).

U.S. Congressman George ("Mickey") Leland, 1983 (photograph courtesy of the Texas Southern University Archives).

The Fifth Ward was a vital center of business and economic activity for blacks, and the businesses located there prospered under the system of segregation that was the norm throughout the South. Despite the adversities and hardships that exist in the area, the community even now continues to make its mark on the social, cultural, and political lives of blacks in the city. Fifth Ward has produced a number of prominent local and national leaders, including U.S. Congresswoman Barbara Jordan, who served from 1972 to 1978, and George "Mickey" Leland, Jordan's immediate successor in the 18th Congressional District, which contains the Fifth Ward.

Though the Fifth Ward once boasted a thriving retail area known as the Lyons Avenue Commercial District, the social and economic vitality of the area was severely disrupted with the completion of two major freeways, Interstate 10 and U.S. 59, which bisected the community. The construction of these two freeway systems created physical barriers that further isolated area residents from the economic core of the Lyons Avenue Commercial District. The community to this day has experienced a steady economic decline. Many businesses have moved out, physical structures are deteriorating, and the population base continues to decrease because of emigration of the younger and more affluent residents. Crime has also contributed to the atmosphere of abandonment and urban decay in what is sometimes called the "Bloody Fifth"; this climate has discouraged new business investments that are urgently needed in the neighborhood.[22]

The Fifth Ward is included among Houston's target areas for both economic development and community development (although there were no specific plans on the drawing board in 1985). While the area is characterized by economic stagnation and deterioration, there is a strong determination on the part of the residents to survive as a neighborhood.[23] A number of positive signs exist in the Fifth Ward. For example, the area has (1) a substantial network of neighborhood institutions that have strong traditional ties to the residents (for example, more than seventy churches, nine public schools, eleven private and public day-care facilities, three medical facilities, and two senior citizens' centers); (2) a core of experienced grass-roots leadership; and (3) a sizable number of black-owned businesses.[24]

The decline of the Fourth and Fifth wards allowed the Third Ward to become the hub of black social, cultural, and economic life in Houston, and the Third Ward now serves as the financial center of black Houston. Specifically, there were two black-owned banks in Texas in 1983; one of the two, Riverside Bank, was located in the heart of Houston's Third Ward. Texas had only one black savings and loan association, Standard Savings, in 1983; it is located in the Third Ward as well. The Houston Citizens Chamber of Commerce moved from the Fourth Ward in 1965 to Wheeler Street in the Third Ward, following the shift in black business concentration. The Houston Citizens Chamber of Commerce represented more than 2,387 local black businesses in 1982.[25]

In addition to being the financial and business center of black Houston, Third Ward serves as a center of black higher education, with the nation's third largest historically black university, Texas Southern University, located there; black mass communications, with the three leading black Houston newspapers and the three black-owned radio stations; and black cultural, civil rights, and political awareness organizations' headquarters located in the Third Ward.[26]

Without doubt, Houston's Third Ward is a neighborhood of contrasts, ranging from dilapidated "shotgun" row houses to well-manicured, tree-lined estates. Though mostly black, this neighborhood in recent years has experienced the in-migration of affluent whites, whose rediscovery of this near-town neighborhood has intensified the competition between incumbent residents and new "urban pioneers" for the area's limited stock of housing. The external pressures exerted on the neighborhood will provide the ultimate test of the Third Ward residents' resourcefulness and ability to mobilize for action in an effort to preserve their area's integrity as a neighborhood.

3.

Housing Occupancy Trends
and Black Neighborhoods

Home ownership is an integral part of the American dream for whites as well as blacks. However, home ownership is not equally distributed among racial groups and social classes. To be sure, the rate of black home ownership continues to lag behind that of whites. Black home ownership in 1980 was 44 percent, compared with 67 percent for whites. Among census regions, southern blacks have the highest rate of home ownership of blacks nationwide, with one-half being home owners; this rate compares with a low of 31 percent in the Northeast.[1]

Home ownership rates increase substantially as families move up the socioeconomic ladder. For those blacks who have incomes greater than $20,000, nearly three-fourths own their own homes, as compared with the 85 percent home ownership rate for all households (whites and blacks combined) with comparable incomes.[2]

The national median income more than doubled between 1967 and 1979, but the price of homes tripled over the same period. Nationally, median prices of homes rose from $20,000 in 1967 to more than $60,000 in 1979. The increased demand for single-family homes escalated the prices of new homes beyond the reach of many Houstonians. Nevertheless, the demand was still strong during the 1970–80 period, thus compounding the problem of inflated home prices. For example, in 1980, if a Houston household did not have an annual income of $25,000, the average home was out of reach.[3] The housing market during the 1970–80 period was a seller's market, with demand exceeding the supply of available housing. However, beginning in the early eighties, housing prices in Houston began to level off, and by the mid-eighties prices actually had declined. The mid-eighties saw Houston's housing market become a buyer's market. Home prices plummeted as a result of the depressed energy prices and resultant sluggish local economy. The oversupply of unsold homes, new and previously owned houses alike, made single-family homes more affordable.

The growth of housing units by census regions indicates that the South added more units than any other area of the country, with more than 2.9 million housing units. The West added 2.5 million units, the North Central region added 1.3 million units, and the Northeast added only 359,000 units in the seventies. The South, since 1965, has accounted for about 40 percent of all the new housing construction in the nation.[4]

Statistics on housing growth within the nation's Standard Metropolitan Statistical Areas (SMSAs) during the seventies also reveal that major gains were made in the southern and western Sunbelt areas. Three Texas metropolitan areas were among the top fifteen SMSAs for housing units constructed between 1970 and 1980. The Houston SMSA led the nation in housing starts during this period, with more than 487,000 new housing units. Dallas–Fort Worth was second, adding more than 364,000 new housing units to the inventory, and the San Antonio SMSA came in twelfth, with 125,000 new units.

BLACK OCCUPANCY TRENDS

The housing boom of the seventies passed over many lower-income and minority neighborhoods. As previously mentioned, black home ownership is indeed higher in the Sunbelt areas, and Houston has a relatively high percentage of black home owners compared with other Southern cities (see Table 3.1). However, the boom in new housing construction that prevailed in the South during the seventies occurred primarily in the wide-open suburbs. The increasing cost of housing during that period narrowed the body of potential buyers to primarily middle-income whites and existing home owners, who had acquired equity capital to finance down payments. As a result, housing starts in central-city areas, where 55 percent of the nation's black households are located, dropped from 36 percent of all housing starts in 1970 to only 29 percent in 1978. The black population continues to be affected by this uneven housing construction pattern, as well as such practices as redlining by banks and mortgage companies, racial steering by real estate firms and leasing

Table 3.1. Black Home Ownership Rates in Selected Southern
Metropolitan Areas, 1980.

SMSA	Total Black Households	Percent Black Home Owners
Houston	170,696	47.2
New Orleans	121,627	35.2
Memphis	108,113	47.3
Atlanta	161,191	41.8
Dallas–Fort Worth	132,925	46.6

Source: U.S. Bureau of the Census, *State and Metropolitan Data Book, 1982* (Washington, D.C.:
Government Printing Office, 1982), table A.

agents, and disparities in capital improvements and amenities between
the central city and the suburbs. Against the backdrop of the thriving
Sunbelt suburbs, the stock of black-owned homes in Southern cities became proportionately older. Black neighborhoods thus ended the boom
decade of the seventies in a state of physical decline.[5]

BLACK SUBURBANIZATION

Blacks who make the move to the suburbs do fare better than their
central-city counterparts in terms of living in newer and better housing. However, blacks still constitute less than 6 percent of the nation's
suburban population. Black suburban occupancy trends indicate that
(1) black home buyers are less likely than white buyers of suburban
homes to have equity capital from previous home sales, (2) black-owned
suburban housing units are more likely than white-owned housing units
to yield lower equity returns upon transfer to another household, and
(3) black-owned suburban homes are more likely than white-owned suburban homes to shift to renter occupancy. Recent housing trends suggest
that as the market tightens, choices may become more limited. This is
true in the central cities as well as in the suburbs. These mobility patterns for lower- and moderate-income blacks point to resegregation or
"reghettoization" of this group—away from the traditional inner-city
neighborhoods and into smaller suburban enclaves.[6]

Although blacks are moving to the suburbs in larger numbers, no national trend of black suburbanization has been clearly demonstrated.
The data in Table 3.2 show population changes in five southern metropolitan areas and their suburbs in 1980. Houston's black population grew
by more than 39 percent in the seventies. During this same period, how-

Table 3.2. Black Population Change in Five Southern Cities and
Their Suburbs, 1970–80.

Central Cities	Black Population 1980	Percent Change in Black Population 1970–80	Percent Black in Central City 1970	1980
Houston	440,257	39.1	25.7	27.6
New Orleans	308,136	15.3	45.0	55.3
Memphis	307,702	26.9	38.9	47.6
Atlanta	282,912	12.1	51.3	66.6
Dallas	266,000	26.3	24.9	29.4

Suburbs	Black Population 1980	Percent Change in Black Population 1970–80	Percent Black in Suburbs 1970	1980
Houston	80,000	21.4	8.8	6.2
New Orleans	79,000	40.4	12.5	12.6
Memphis	37,000	−18.4	31.7	21.0
Atlanta	179,000	222.4	6.2	14.2
Dallas	50,000	35.4	5.2	4.7

Source: U.S. Bureau of the Census, *Census of Population and Housing,* 1981.

ever, the black share of Houston's suburban population actually de-
clined, from 8.8 percent in 1970 to 6.2 percent in 1980; the decrease
was a result of the white suburban population's much faster growth. This
trend of decreasing black suburban population is not new in the Houston
area; in 1960 blacks made up nearly 13 percent of Houston's suburban
population. The 80,000 blacks in Houston's suburbs in 1980 represented
a smaller number by far than might be expected from the size of the
central city black population of more than 400,000.[7]

Atlanta's blacks, unlike their Houston counterparts, established a
well-defined migration stream to the suburbs during the 1970s. The
city's black suburban population increased by more than 222 percent between 1970 and 1980 and comprised more than 14 percent of the suburban Atlanta population in 1980. Likewise, the black suburban population in the New Orleans and Dallas–Fort Worth metropolitan areas grew
by 40 and 35 percent, respectively. Memphis, on the other hand, experienced a dramatic decrease in numbers of black suburban residents.
The black share of Memphis's suburban population dropped from nearly
32 percent in 1970 to 21 percent in 1980.

Although black suburbanization has generally meant an upgrading in
housing for these blacks, it has also meant successive "spillover" from

black neighborhoods—an extension of the segregated housing pattern that is typical of the central city. Suburban neighborhoods that were racially integrated in the seventies often have become predominantly black neighborhoods in the eighties. This pattern is typified in southeast and northeast Houston residential areas. From the beginning, though, there were some black enclaves to be found on the periphery of the city. These neighborhoods—such as Carverdale, Blue Ridge, Acres Homes, Sunnyside, Settegast, Pleasantville, Galena Manor, and Carvercrest— share a history of municipal neglect, but residents have developed strong loyalties to these areas.[8]

GROWTH AND THE INNER CITY

The black housing patterns in Houston can be traced directly to the long-established segregated and often isolated neighborhoods in the inner city and on the suburban fringe. The city's black population expanded outward from the Third, Fourth, and Fifth wards (see Map 3.1). Many of these older inner-city neighborhoods suffered during the city's rapid expansion through the aggressive annexation of surrounding areas. A 1979 report from the Mayor's Urban Policy Advisory Board summarized the plight of many of Houston's inner-city neighborhoods: "Houston has grown alarmingly fast. . . . While this burgeoning growth has maintained Houston's healthy economic independence, it has also been responsible for the focus of City services in newer neighborhoods at the expense of most inner-city neighborhoods."[9]

Sociologist Henry A. Bullock described the dynamics of Houston's black neighborhoods in the 1950s:

> These areas are more than mere geographical locations. They are places where Negroes live, symbolizing the complexity of feelings aroused by associations connected with the location people call "home." People of one area associate more with each other than with people of other areas. Their loyalty toward each other is stronger, and they are definitely oriented toward their areas in terms of more immediate needs. Each area is pierced by a main street which acts as a focal point around which commercial and recreational activities whirl. Dowling Street of Third Ward; West Dallas of Fourth; and Lyons Avenue of Fifth Ward are three of the main streets toward which areal orientation is sharpest.[10]

Many of the city's black inner-city neighborhoods continue to lose residents as well as a substantial portion of their housing stock for

Map 3.1. Predominantly black Houston neighborhoods, 1982. (Base map by Key Maps, Inc., lic. no. 93.)

1. **Third Ward**
2. **Fourth Ward**
3. **Fifth Ward**
4. **Foster Place/ MacGregor**
5. **West End**
6. **Kashmere Gardens**
7. **Pleasantville**
8. **Clinton Park**
9. **Sunnyside**
10. **South Park**
11. **Almeda Plaza**
12. **Hiram Clarke**
13. **Chasewood**
14. **Briargate**
15. **Riceville**
16. **Carvercrest- Pineypoint**
17. **Carverdale**
18. **Acres Homes**
19. **Shepherd Park**
20. **Studewood Heights**
21. **Settegast**
22. **Trinity Gardens**
23. **Scenic Woods**
24. **Northwood Manor**
25. **Bordersville**

lower- and moderate-income households. Neighborhood decline is manifested in the increasing number of boarded-up and abandoned buildings and empty lots that dot many of Houston's inner-city neighborhoods. It is no wonder, then, that lower-income and elderly persons find themselves trapped in the city's poverty pockets, where housing is most affordable. Limited income is the major factor preventing residents in these areas from competing for housing on the open market. Thus, families with limited financial means are caught between rising housing costs and a dwindling supply of decent and affordable housing in Houston's inner-city areas.

Many psychological barriers once associated with inner-city neighborhoods are gradually being lifted in selected close-in neighborhoods. This has created the phenomenon of gentrification, in which younger, usually white, home buyers find housing bargains by investing "sweat equity" and repair costs in older, inner-city houses. The rising costs of owning and operating an automobile, new housing construction, and previously owned homes, and the desire to live in classic, sophisticated urban neighborhoods rather than in the monotonous suburbs to which the previous generation had fled have accelerated the appearance of middle- and upper-income enclaves in many cities.[11] Neighborhoods have been revitalized and made attractive to other potential buyers, and lower-income residents have been displaced because of the higher property values and higher costs that result from increased demand for these homes. As in other cities, Houston's close-in neighborhoods have become hot in the real-estate market, and racial and ethnic exclusion has resulted as demand boosts prices in the neighborhoods that the minority residents had inherited in the white flight to the suburbs.[12]

Thus, the fears and anxieties of being displaced from one's home (whether real or imagined) are rife in many black neighborhoods. Residents feel threatened by the city's favorable posture toward neighborhood preservation and revitalization. A classic example of fear generated by redevelopment plans is Houston's Fourth Ward—to be sure a neighborhood under siege. The fate of one of Houston's oldest black neighborhoods is uncertain because of the small number of owner-occupied housing units in the area. The residents of the Fourth Ward are vulnerable to residential displacement, inasmuch as the vast majority are renters. As blacks gradually lost ownership of the land in what was once Freedmen's Town, they also lost essential leverage in determining the future of the neighborhood. First of all, the neighborhood is adjacent to the central business district and occupies some of the most valuable property in the city. Moreover, the neighborhood has been allowed to deteriorate over the years. No doubt extreme pressure will be brought to bear on the Fourth Ward when developers and the absentee property owners feel that the time is right for redeveloping the area.

Four events in the early 1980s can be seen as signals that the time is near for the redevelopment of the severely neglected Fourth Ward: (1) the decision by the Houston Housing Authority to demolish the Allen Parkway Village public housing project, which covers more than thirty-seven acres; (2) the decision by the Harris County Hospital district to relocate its medical services from Jefferson Davis Hospital (a public health facility) to a new hospital to be constructed in northeast Houston; (3) the creation of the Fourth Ward Property Owners Association; and (4) the decision by Houston's City Planning Department to take the lead in designing "mini-plans" for the redevelopment of the Fourth Ward neighborhood. In addition, the Environmental Protection Agency's ban in the 1970s on development in the inner city (the area bounded by Loop 610 freeway)—the so-called "sewer moratorium," enacted to prevent further overflows of sewage into the bayous—was finally lifted, and this action appeared likely to accelerate the development process in the neighborhood. Specifically, the completion of the city's Sixty-ninth Street Sewage Treatment Plant greatly increased the capacity for new development in the inner city. The combined impact of these factors is likely to trigger future development activity in the Fourth Ward.

The residents of Houston's black neighborhoods share a common struggle of trying to maintain a sense of residential stability, to improve the quality of housing and municipal services, and to minimize displacement of residents. The gentrification of many inner-city neighborhoods has placed extreme pressures on residents of these areas. Black, lower-income, elderly, and renter households were disproportionately represented among the individuals displaced from revitalized inner-city neighborhoods, yet they represented only a small share of the residents of suburbia, where the bulk of the single-family homes were built in the seventies. Blacks who made the move from the central city found themselves resegregated in the suburbs. Many of the problems once associated with life in the central city, such as crowding, neighborhood decline, and inadequate municipal services, are problems that confront more and more black suburban residents.

4.

Housing the City's Poor

Low- and moderate-income families continue to have problems finding suitable housing in the Houston area. Federally subsidized housing for the poor has been surrounded by controversy since its establishment during the Roosevelt New Deal administration. The U.S. Housing Act of 1937 and subsequent state legislation led to the establishment of the Housing Authority of the City of Houston (HACH), which was responsible for the construction of housing for low-income families under the low-rent housing program established by the Housing Act of 1937. A two-pronged approach was used in carrying out the mission of the HACH: (1) to clear slums and blighted areas and (2) to provide decent, safe, and sanitary housing.[1] The HACH is the largest of the forty public housing authorities in the Houston-Galveston metropolitan area.

The need for additional housing for Houston's low- and moderate-income families has grown by more than 200 percent during the period from 1978 to 1983. However, the number of available housing units for this group showed only a modest increase for that five-year period. Specifically, in 1978 there were 8,702 housing units in the city that were receiving some type of housing subsidy. The number of subsidized housing units increased to 9,584 in 1982 and to 9,893 in 1983.[2] A breakdown of the HACH's units in 1983 shows that it owned and managed 4,077 units of public housing in fifteen developments scattered across the city. The housing authority's Housing Assistance Payments Program (sometimes informally referred to as the Section 8 housing program) provided rent subsidies for an additional 5,816 units.[3] The HACH, in all, served more than 25,000 persons in 1983.

The need for additional units of low-rent and assisted housing in Houston far exceeds the supply. The city's Community Development Office estimated in 1979 that at least one-fifth of the city's 600,000 households were inadequately housed and could qualify for some type of housing assistance.[4] As a result, the HACH had more than 5,000 families on its public housing waiting list for a five-year period (1980–85).

Houston's aging and rapidly deteriorating supply of public housing represents an additional problem to the housing authority in its effort to provide decent, safe, and sanitary housing for low- and moderate-income households. The challenge of operating and maintaining the existing public housing stock while trying to establish additional housing for the poor creates a dilemma that many cities face. These problems are exacerbated by dwindling financial resources and decreasing political support for low-income housing. Furthermore, controversy frequently surrounds the selection of sites for public housing projects. Residents of middle-income neighborhoods often object to the building of public housing developments in their areas, arguing that such developments adversely affect the quality of life in their neighborhoods.

CONVENTIONAL PUBLIC HOUSING PROJECTS

The construction of conventional public housing projects in Houston has always been mired in controversy. The early members of the city's Housing Authority Board often emphasized the "slum clearance" provision of their charge rather than the provision for constructing housing for the poor. Land acquisition for public housing projects was also at the heart of the controversy. The *Houston Post* in 1940 reported on allegations and charges that the city's Housing Authority Board used "slum clearance to capitalize [on] poverty and drive a bargain" in Houston's blighted neighborhoods.[5]

Conventional public housing construction received a major setback in 1950 when Houston voters approved a measure that would limit the number of public housing units. As a result, few public housing developments were built in Houston between 1952 and 1975. That 1950 referendum is a major contributing factor in the current shortage of low- and moderate-income public housing stock in Houston. The supply of public housing units in Houston is smaller than that of cities of comparable size, as indicated in Table 4.1. Although Houston was the nation's fourth largest city in 1982, it ranked seventh in the number of public housing units. Houston and Philadelphia are comparable in size, but Philadelphia has more than twice as many public housing units as Houston.

Table 4.1. Number of Public Housing Units in the Ten Largest U.S. Cities, 1982.

City	No. of Units	Ranking of Units by Size	Ranking of Population by Size[a]
New York	207,648	1	1
Los Angeles	26,000	3	2
Chicago	47,000	2	3
Houston	9,500	7	4
Philadelphia	23,000	4	5
Detroit	10,500	6	6
San Antonio	14,000	5	7
Dallas	8,000	8	8
Phoenix	1,800	9	9
San Diego	340	10	10

Source: *Houston Chronicle,* August 8, 1982.
[a] Unofficial population ranking in 1982.

Table 4.2. Public Housing Authority Developments in Houston, 1983.

Development	Houston Location	Number of Units	Percent Black in Census Tract[a]
Family			
Allen Parkway Village	Southwest	1,000	63.4
Clayton Homes	Southeast	348	17.3
Cuney Homes	Southeast	564	99.4
Ewing	Southeast	42	47.2
Forest Green	Northeast	100	78.8
Irvington Village	Northwest	318	6.2
Kelly Village	Northeast	333	94.3
Kennedy Place	Northeast	60	94.3
Lincoln Park	Northwest	264	60.6
Long Drive	Southeast	100	1.3
Oxford Place	Northwest	230	4.3
Wilmington House	Southeast	108	99.5
Elderly			
Bellerive	Southwest	210	4.7
Lyerly	Northwest	200	56.5
Telephone Road	Southeast	200	35.4

Source: Housing Authority of the City of Houston, *Annual Report,* 1983.
[a] Percentages are based on 1980 Census figures.

San Antonio, which is smaller in population than Houston, has some forty-five hundred more public housing units than Houston.

The locations of the HACH's fifteen developments are given in Table 4.2. Black neighborhoods continue to contain a substantial number of the city's public housing developments (eight of the fifteen). This situation can be traced to the historical policy of racially segregated housing. Houston's City Planning Department in the 1920s strongly suggested that segregated housing be the official policy of the city, and, in 1939, Cuney Homes was built for blacks. In 1941, the HACH constructed Kelly Village to house blacks and Allen Parkway Village for whites only. Other early public housing in Houston continued to reflect the segregation policy and was located in black neighborhoods. However, the U.S. Department of Housing and Urban Development (HUD) established in the 1970s a new policy of "spatial deconcentration," which limits the number of public housing units that can be built in minority and low-income neighborhoods. The HUD site criterion has led to the construction of public housing units in "non-concentrated," that is, suburban, areas. The intent behind this was to move public housing tenants closer to employment centers, many of which have shifted to suburban areas, and to provide tenants with the amenities available in suburban areas, such as better schools, recreational facilities, and shopping areas.

There is also a discernible pattern in the location of the developments for families and for the elderly. In Houston the public housing developments that are designed for families are mostly located in the eastern half of the city, while the three developments for the elderly are located in every quadrant of the city except the northeast. Although there are four family developments in the western quadrants, three of them are in minority neighborhoods. The geographic locations of future public housing developments in the city continue to be influenced by public opinion. It is far easier to get public housing designed for the elderly constructed than it is to get family developments constructed. The ethnic composition of the low-income elderly versus the low-income families largely determines the acceptance or rejection of proposed developments in the suburban areas. Houston's housing developments for the elderly have predominantly white tenant populations, while the low-income family developments tend to be occupied by black, Hispanic, and Indochinese tenants.[6]

The issue of where public housing "should" be located, that is, the inner city versus the suburbs, has become a volatile political issue. Black inner-city residents fear that public housing developments are being programmed for systematic elimination through the policy of neglect and site location away from the people who need public housing the most—the lower-income families in the inner city. On the other side of the issue, white suburbanites fear that their neighborhoods will be targets for lower-income housing projects because of the federal government's policy limiting the construction of new subsidized housing units in minority neighborhoods. A case in point is the 1982 decision by the HACH to approve the construction of two housing developments designed for families in two white middle-class neighborhoods. The housing authority approved the construction of a $5-million, 105-unit low-income housing development in southwest Houston, in the Westbury area, where the census tract showed a racial composition of 89 percent white, 4 percent black, and 7 percent Hispanic. The selection of this mostly white neighborhood in southwest Houston sparked protests, demonstrations, and legal action. The project was ultimately shelved after the developer had problems securing the $5-million loan approval to begin construction.

A similar case of political and public pressure applied to halt the construction of low-income housing involved a proposed project in northwest Houston. A $3.5-million, eighty-unit public housing development was approved in 1982 by the HACH for the Spring Branch area. The census tract in which the low-income housing development was to be located was 87 percent white, 4 percent black, and 9 percent Hispanic. Area residents were able to garner enough support from county and state elected officials to convince the developer not to purchase the land for the proposed project. The housing authority subsequently canceled the controversial low-income family development.

Public opposition to low-income housing construction in "non-concentrated" areas of the city appears to be increasing. The successful Westbury and Spring Branch protests against the first two attempts by the housing authority to locate family developments in areas that were not historically minority neighborhoods meant that the potential 185 low-income family units were not added to the city's already inadequate supply of public housing. The HACH ended up trying to salvage some of the federal funds allocated to those ill-fated projects by proposing to build a complex for the elderly in the Westbury area, with the idea that the elderly would be more acceptable to the white neighborhood.[7]

Blacks constituted a majority in four of the five family developments that the HACH administered in 1976, with Hispanics being the majority in the fifth family development. The largest black concentrations in family developments were found in Kelly Village (Fifth Ward), Cuney Homes (Third Ward), and Allen Parkway Village (Fourth Ward). The largest concentration of Hispanics in the city's family developments was found in Irvington Village (near northside). Two family developments, Clayton Homes and Allen Parkway Village, had small Indochinese popu-

Table 4.3. Ethnic Composition of Houston Housing Authority
Developments, August, 1984.

Housing Development	No. of Units	Percent Black	Percent Hispanic	Percent White	Percent Oriental/ Other	Percent Black in Census Tract[a]
Family						
Allen Parkway Village	1,000	34.1	2.8	5.0	58.1	63.4
Clayton Homes	348	47.3	32.0	0.4	20.3	17.3
Cuney Homes	564	98.9	0.4	0.1	0.6	99.4
Irvington Village	318	28.9	60.2	9.9	1.0	6.2
Kelly Village	333	96.1	0.9	0.0	3.0	94.3
Lincoln Park	264	99.3	0.7	0.0	0.0	0.6
Oxford Place	230	87.9	6.5	5.1	0.5	4.3
Forest Green	100	100.0	0.0	0.0	0.0	78.8
Ewing	42	87.5	2.5	7.5	2.5	47.2
Kennedy Place	60	89.8	3.4	0.0	6.8	94.3
Wilmington House	108	98.1	0.0	0.0	1.9	99.5
Long Drive	100	74.0	22.0	3.0	1.0	1.3
Elderly						
75 Lyerly	200	16.2	19.7	64.1	0.0	56.5
Bellerive	210	5.7	20.0	72.9	1.4	4.7
Telephone Road	200	18.1	9.0	70.9	2.0	35.4

Source: Housing Authority of the City of Houston Calculations, Houston Housing Authority.
[a]Census tract data are based on the 1980 U.S. Census.

lations in 1976. On the other hand, the public housing developments for elderly persons were largely occupied by whites; nine of every ten units for the elderly were occupied by a white household in 1976.

A 1984 description of the HACH's fifteen housing developments indicated that minority group members continued to constitute a majority of the project tenants (Table 4.3). Blacks were a majority in nine of the twelve family developments. Hispanic public housing tenants continued to be concentrated in Irvington Village, with smaller numbers of Hispanic families housed in the city's other family developments. The most dramatic change that occurred in the city's public housing between 1976 and 1984 was the rapid increase in Oriental public housing tenants, mostly Indochinese refugees, in two family developments: Allen Parkway Village and Clayton Homes.

Beginning in 1976 there appears to have been a "replacement" policy on the part of the HACH for Allen Parkway Village, that is, Indochinese rather than blacks would be selected for placement in the development. The black tenant population dropped from 66 percent in 1976 to 34 per-

Table 4.4. Ethnic Composition of Allen Parkway Village for Selected Years.

Year	Percent Black	Percent Hispanic	Percent White	Percent Oriental/ Other
1976	66.0	3.0	26.0	5.0
1980	45.8	2.3	10.9	41.0
1983	33.1	2.0	6.9	58.3
1984	34.1	2.8	5.0	58.1

Source: Housing Authority of the City of Houston, Housing Management Division, *Allen Parkway Village Summary Reports*, 1984.

cent in 1984. This policy was also a likely contributor to the increase in the Indochinese population in Clayton Homes, though to a lesser degree.

Because physical conditions at Allen Parkway Village have been allowed to deteriorate severely, so that most of the units are not suitable for habitation, the project has become the subject of much speculation, and its cloudy future may put the future of the entire Fourth Ward at risk. The commonly held belief around this black community in the shadow of the central business district is that "as Allen Parkway Village goes, so goes the Fourth Ward."[8] As the project's condition worsens and fewer units are habitable (only 528 of the 1,000 units were occupied in August, 1984[9]) it becomes an easier target for redevelopment. And with the gradual replacement of black tenants with Indochinese refugees, especially from 1976 to 1980 (see Table 4.4), in Allen Parkway Village, that community focus of the Fourth Ward was no longer black. Thus, both situations may serve to erase the historic Fourth Ward.

DECENT HOUSING VIA SECTION 8

Numerous attempts have been made since the 1950s to alleviate the housing problems of the poor. With the passage of the Housing and Community Development Act of 1974, the Section 8 housing program was initiated. This provision means that low-income families will be housed in designated privately owned buildings, which ordinarily would have prohibitively high rents for such families. The owners of housing in the program receive funds from the federal government to supplement rents from low-income tenants. The federal government pays a subsidy equal to the difference between the rents that low-income families can afford and federally certified fair-market rents for the housing units. The Section 8 housing program's income eligibility guidelines are designed so that a family pays no more than one-fourth of its income for rent. The goals of the Section 8 housing program were to (1) improve the quality of housing available to the economically disadvantaged, (2) foster ethnic/racial and economic integration, and (3) increase the disposable income of the nation's poor by providing low-cost, secure, and decent housing. An attempt was made to measure the success of the Section 8 program in Houston in making affordable housing in ethnically and economically mixed areas available to low-income persons.[10] The study's data included personal interviews with 200 current housing allowance recipients. Of the respondents interviewed, 104 were "nonmovers" (recipients who had resided in their current housing prior to receiving rental assistance), and 96 were "movers" (recipients who had relocated to their current housing upon receiving the rent subsidy). The ethnic composition of the sample included 118 blacks (59 percent), 68 whites (24 percent), and 14 Hispanics (7 percent).

Section 8 has provisions that allow eligible participants to select housing in the neighborhoods of their choosing, provided that the rent does not exceed the fair-market rent allowed. Even with such provisions, the historical patterns of segregation continue to operate in the housing search and selection processes. Data in Table 4.5 indicate that minority tenants continue to live in census tracts that are heavily populated by minorities. Similarly, white participants secure housing in predominantly white areas.

Overall, Houston's Section 8 housing tenants have leased housing in neighborhoods where their own ethnic group predominates. Thus, for

Table 4.5. Distribution of Tenants in Census Tracts by Ethnicity, 1978.

Percentage of Minorities in Tracts[a]	Nonmovers				Movers				Total	
	Minority		White		Minority		White			
	N[b]	Percent	N	Percent	N	Percent	N	Percent	N	Percent
Less than 10	4	(6.2)	23	(57.5)	3	(4.4)	12	(42.9)	42	(21.0)
10–29	6	(9.4)	13	(32.4)	6	(8.8)	12	(42.9)	37	(18.5)
30–49	2	(3.1)	1	(2.5)	2	(2.9)	1	(3.5)	6	(3.0)
50–69	2	(3.1)	1	(2.5)	9	(13.2)	1	(3.5)	13	(6.5)
70–89	14	(21.9)	2	(5.0)	12	(17.7)	0	(0.0)	28	(14.0)
90+	36	(56.3)	0	(0.0)	36	(53.0)	2	(7.2)	74	(37.0)
Total	64	(100.0)	40	(100.0)	68	(100.0)	28	(100.0)	200	(100.0)

[a] Percentages based on the 1970 Census.
[b] N = number.

the most part, the local housing allowance program has had a minimal effect in reversing the trend of ethnic and racial segregation, a key ingredient in the Section 8 housing program's thrust. Framers of the housing allowance program also sought to facilitate the entrance of lower-income families into traditionally middle-income dwelling units and neighborhoods.

One means of assessing the extent to which the program has provided housing for the poor in areas with low- or moderate-income, multi- or single-family housing is to compare the tenants' housing in relation to surrounding neighborhood poverty. Less than 10 percent of the minority households in a sample were located in tracts with significantly low poverty levels (less than 5 percent poverty). However, more than 40 percent of the white tenants surveyed lived in areas where less than 5 percent of the families were below the poverty level. When the minority movers' and nonmovers' housing locations are compared, more than 60 percent of the minority tenants who relocated settled in tracts where 15 to 34 percent of the households were below the poverty line. However, a large percentage (73 percent) of the minority tenants who elected not to move were found in tracts where there was a substantial level of poverty (15 to 34 percent).

Federal housing officials designed the Section 8 housing program as an alternative to conventional public housing developments, which were often located in densely populated, low-income minority neighborhoods. In addition to its goal of being cost-effective, the Section 8 housing program was intended to facilitate both ethnic and economic integration of its participants. This goal was to be accomplished by allowing low-income and minority participants to compete for standard rental units in middle-income areas. Initially introduced nationally as a demonstration program, Section 8 has been institutionalized as one of the largest housing programs for the poor.

The Section 8 program became a popular program for low-income rental assistance because the bulk of the housing units were located in existing apartment complexes. Moreover, newly constructed Section 8 units were built in standard housing developments with a portion reserved for low-income, disabled, and elderly renters. Very little controversy surrounded the existing or newly constructed Section 8 housing units since the problem of site selection and the stigma of a "housing project" were not present. Although the Section 8 housing program has fallen short of its goal of integration, it has emerged as one of the few low-income housing programs that is not surrounded by controversy and citizen opposition. This program provides a large share of the housing for the nation's urban poor in an era when conventional public housing projects are being scaled down through the shrinking operating subsidies provided by the federal government.

Houston, like other major cities, will suffer if its public housing inventory drops from its current level. Long waiting lists and the growing problem of homelessness are clear indicators of the need for additional low- and moderate-income assisted housing. However, public housing developments are in such a state of disrepair that many are collapsing under their own weight. This problem exists from coast to coast.

The commitment to public housing has weakened over the years. Public housing was never meant to be permanent housing for the poor, but was created as temporary housing for the "submerged middle-class," a group that was poor because of the Great Depression and has evolved over the years into permanent housing for mostly low-income and minority households. The local and federal commitment to public housing has shifted with these changing demographics. Cutbacks in operating subsidies and rising costs of maintaining low-income housing developments have left many housing authorities with extreme fiscal problems that are not likely to abate in the near future.

5.

The Persisting Barrier
of Discrimination in Housing

Discrimination in the housing industry has denied a basic form of investment to a significant segment of American society. Even though the federal Fair Housing Act of 1968 prohibited racial discrimination in housing, blacks still do not receive equal treatment in the market or enjoy complete freedom of choice in housing. Nearly every major American city has created a fair housing division to monitor and implement fair housing policies, but the facts indicate that these agencies have had only varying success in reducing discrimination.

The tax law provisions for home ownership provide benefits of more than $15 billion per year.[1] However, institutionalized racism in the housing market severely restricts blacks' home ownership options and thereby denies them the benefits of tax savings and long-term investments. Institutionalized racism can include such practices as refusing to sell or lease housing to blacks, coding records and applications to indicate racial preferences of landlords, selective advertising, threats or acts of intimidation, racial steering (when real estate agents show minority clients homes only in minority or low-income areas), and redlining (when lenders establish policies of not making loans for homes in low-income and minority areas of the city).[2]

Even the federal commitment to the enforcement of fair housing laws appears to have weakened.[3] Financial and manpower support necessary to pursue and rigorously enforce fair housing policies has been inadequate. In fact, there is a growing sentiment at the federal level that special efforts are no longer needed to ensure equal opportunity in housing. Civil rights violations in the area of fair housing continue to go uncorrected, underscoring the low priority accorded to federal enforcement of the current fair housing laws. The U.S. Commission on Civil Rights

arrived at the following conclusion on the status of fair housing enforcement efforts: "Title VII of the Civil Rights act of 1968, the primary federal fair housing law, does not provide effective enforcement
mechanisms for ensuring fair housing. Those federal departments and
agencies charged with ensuring equal housing opportunity have not adequately carried out this duty. The government's appropriations in support of fair housing have been inadequate to meet the nation's needs in
this critical area of civil rights."[4]

Thus, the court rulings and legislation that were fought for over the
years have not ended the impediments to freedom of choice for all
Americans in finding a place to live, and there is clear evidence that fair
housing laws have not been enforced by the same means used to obtain
compliance with other laws.[5] A 1979 report by the U.S. Department of
Housing and Urban Development covered a study of forty metropolitan
areas. For the study, black "testers" set out to secure specific housing,
followed by white testers seeking the same housing that the black testers
had been refused. The statistics based on the agents' behavior showed
that more than 27 percent of the rental agents and 15 percent of the sales
agents had practiced some form of housing discrimination. However,
the level of discrimination blacks reported experiencing in their housing
search revealed that one of every two blacks had encountered some form
of housing discrimination.[6]

The problem of housing discrimination in the nation's cities is likely
to worsen as available housing in "quality" neighborhoods becomes
scarce.[7] The search for decent and affordable housing by the nation's
baby-boom generation has stressed an already constricted housing market. For this large group of adults, housing took on special social and
political significance. This generation, better educated and earning more
than their parents did, were still often unable to afford the kind of home
their parents had considered a right rather than a privilege, and thus the
baby boomers could not achieve the American dream. The nation's housing shortage, that is to say, shortage of moderate-income housing, has
forced many of these young "nesters" to alter their expectations and to
move into lower-quality housing located in transitional neighborhoods,
where dwelling units are changing, from single-family to multifamily,
for example.[8] This process is occurring at the same time that "no-
children" policies in rental housing are on the increase; one in four
rental units did not allow children in 1980, as compared with one in six,
prior to 1975.[9]

Housing developers appear to have responded to the national decline in family size and the rise in the number of childless households. They have responded by building apartment complexes with the one-bedroom apartment as the standard unit. However, minority households continue to be larger and are more likely to have children present than the national average. Differences in home ownership rates between minorities and whites affect housing type. More than one-half of minority families are confined to the renter market as compared with one-third of the nation's whites. If a family is large, a member of an ethnic minority, female-headed, or has children present, the chances of being poorly housed are increased substantially. Exclusionary and restrictive policies against families with children are greatest in high-quality residential areas that are characterized by recently constructed units with high monthly rents and a predominantly white population, and so minority households are affected by these policies more than white households.[10]

DISCRIMINATION AND RESIDENTIAL PACKAGES

Two major theoretical models have been developed to explain how residential segregation can produce different housing packages (housing quality plus residential amenities such as neighborhood stability, shopping centers, employment opportunities) for blacks and whites. The first is the equilibrium model, which assumes that residential segregation is caused not by discrimination but by the preferences of those seeking housing; it assumes that, all else being equal, whites prefer to live in white neighborhoods and that blacks prefer to live in integrated neighborhoods. The disequilibrium model, however, is based on the assumption that residential segregation is a direct result of discrimination, which restricts blacks to housing that whites leave or that has been converted from other uses, that is, housing that whites do not want. For example, a large Victorian-style home vacated by whites may be split up into apartments that are smaller and have fewer amenities than standard suburban apartments. In the disequilibrium model, blacks pay inflated prices for such housing because demand for this artificially limited housing stock is high and the owners know this and charge accordingly. But many blacks will pay this "black tax" in order to become home owners.[11]

The spiraling costs of housing that black and other minority families must contend with (as must other Americans) are a heavy burden, especially since they are in addition to individual and institutional discrimination. Two types of discrimination are particularly relevant to the housing patterns of American cities: (1) price discrimination, which refers to the act of charging one group a higher price than another group for identical housing, and (2) exclusion, which refers to any technique designed to avoid selling or renting housing in a given location to a certain group of people.[12]

Because blacks face a restricted housing supply, they pay more than whites of equal income for otherwise identical housing. It has been estimated that a nonwhite family buying a single-family home must pay 5 to 20 percent more for comparable living quarters than a white family does.[13] Other economic and social costs are imposed on blacks. Having to pay more for housing means that a larger share of blacks' incomes (already significantly lower than whites' incomes) must go for housing, leaving even less in the household budget for clothing, food, and other necessities. Also, blacks whose housing options are confined to inner-city areas get less of a return on their tax dollars, as residential services (police and fire protection, street repairs, and so on) have been found again and again to vary significantly according to neighborhood location and racial/ethnic composition. A 1979 study by Franklin Wilson arrived at the following conclusion on the relationship between discrimination and residential housing patterns:

> The main effect of discrimination on the residential behavior of blacks is a restriction on the range of residential packages that blacks may choose from. However, it is clear that low-income black households are most affected by the economic costs of living in segregated neighborhoods. These households are placed at a serious disadvantage when the supply of housing in black neighborhoods is limited because they cannot outbid higher income households for available decent housing. The economic costs borne by middle- and upper-income black households consist mainly of artificially high prices for what they get and restriction of their ability to consume the full range of desirable attributes rather than inability to obtain any acceptable housing at all.[14]

Racial discrimination in housing occurs independent of income. The U.S. Department of Housing and Urban Development reports that lending institutions have a higher rate of rejection of minorities' applications for mortgages than of nonminorities' applications, regardless of income level.[15] The higher rejection rate occurred even when controls were added for the applicants' years on the job, their level of debt, and their total assets. Rejections of minority loan applicants who earned from $15,000 to $25,000 were 50 percent higher than for nonminority loan applicants earning the same amount; more than 25 percent of the minorities with assets of $25,000 to $30,000 were denied loans, as compared with only 12 percent of the nonminority applicants with similar assets. The net effect of these forms of institutionalized discrimination is the creation of two separate housing markets at all rent and price levels: a highly restricted market for racial minorities and an open, choice-filled market for the white majority.[16]

DISCRIMINATION, HOUSTON STYLE

The City of Houston, in an effort to promote "open" housing based on freedom of choice and ability to pay, created its Fair Housing Division. This agency became operational through the city's Fair Housing Ordinance, which was passed on July 9, 1975, nearly seven years after the federal Fair Housing Act of 1968. Houston's ordinance was patterned after the federal fair housing legislation. It prohibited discrimination in the sale, rental, or financing of housing, as well as discrimination in broker services on the basis of race or color, sex, religion, or national origin. The city ordinance was hailed by Mayor Jim McConn as a first step in obtaining a "basic human right" for all citizens. The mayor summarized his views on fair housing as follows: "As a builder, I recognize the need for all people to have access to adequate housing. When certain people are restricted from the housing market because of their race, sex, national origin, or religion, the entire community suffers. A segregated city only serves to defeat itself. This administration is dedicated to the enforcement of the Fair Housing Ordinance and the ideals which it represents."[17]

Nevertheless, the political constituencies for the fair housing efforts have never been a powerful force in Houston. Although the local fair housing ordinance forbids housing discrimination, it suffers from the same problem the federal fair housing legislation does, namely, weak enforcement provisions. For instance, Houston's Fair Housing Ordinance fails to provide the Fair Housing Division with any enforcement powers. The city agency charged with tackling the local housing discrimination problem can seek only voluntary compliance through "conciliation" activities, or formal and informal negotiations. It could also send cases to the city attorney for litigation; the Fair Housing Division was not equipped with its own legal staff to pursue litigation on its own.

The effectiveness of the local fair housing agency has suffered as a result of half-hearted commitment by City Hall, which allowed the size of the agency's staff to fluctuate over the years. On January 1, 1976, the staff included the director, an assistant director, one secretary, and two interns. One year later, the Fair Housing Division had grown to nine full-time employees (four of whom were compliance officers).[18] By September, 1984, the agency's staff was down to three persons: an "acting" director, one compliance officer, and a secretary. In March, 1985, the Fair Housing Division was merged with the city's Affirmative Action Division, thus ending its ten-year history as an autonomous city department. During its decade of independent operation, the agency's office had also been moved several times, further inconveniencing operations and hampering its compliance functions. Moreover, the telephone listing which the agency was originally assigned was changed in 1983. The move and the change in telephone numbers made it difficult for complainants to reach the Fair Housing Division.

Despite the problems of the agency, Houstonians continued to file housing discrimination complaints. For the period 1975 through 1983, the agency received more than 1,767 housing discrimination complaints. Complaint activity fluctuated from year to year, with the greatest number of complaints (478) being filed in 1976, the second year the agency was in operation. The newness of the Fair Housing Division probably contributed to the large number of complaints filed during the initial operation of the program. In the early 1980s the number of complaints dropped off significantly, hovering between 100 and 150 per year.

Expectations were high during the initial years after the passage of the city's Fair Housing Ordinance. However, more recent public sentiment toward the agency was mixed. The key ingredient in the mix of public reaction concerns the question of the agency's effectiveness, specifically, the disposition of complaints. The disposition of local housing discrimination complaints between 1979 and 1982 is presented in Table 5.1. Action taken on complaints filed with the Houston Fair Housing Division fell into one of four categories: (1) formal conciliation, (2) informal conciliation, (3) referral to the city attorney, and (4) dismissal. More than two-thirds of the discrimination complaints filed ended up in category (4). The dismissals were usually for technical reasons such as the lack of the proper signatures on the paperwork, insufficient evidence, or jurisdictional problems (the ordinance applies only to housing inside the Houston city limits). Sometimes applicants withdrew their complaints. The agency used "voluntary" compliance as the chief method of resolving the complaints that were not dismissed. Informal conciliation—getting all concerned parties to sit down in an informal

Table 5.1. Disposition of Housing Discrimination Complaints in Houston, 1979–82.

	Year			
Disposition	*1979*	*1980*	*1981*	*1982*
Formal conciliation	8 (4.6%)	2 (1.7%)	2 (1.7%)	7 (6.7%)
Informal conciliation	32 (18.3%)	41 (34.2%)	38 (32.5%)	35 (33.3%)
Referred to city attorney	3 (1.7%)	1 (0.8%)	1 (0.8%)	1 (0.9%)
Dismissed	132 (75.4%)	76 (63.3%)	76 (65.0%)	62 (59.1%)
Total	175 (100.0%)	120 (100.0%)	117 (100.0%)	105 (100.0%)

Source: City of Houston Fair Housing Division, 1983.

setting and resolve the problem—accounted for more than one-fourth of the complaints disposed of between 1979 and 1982. Only six complaints were referred to the city's legal department for litigation.[19]

The Houston Fair Housing Division records give the geographic location where each complaint originated. Houston is generally thought of as being divided into quadrants—northeast, northwest, southeast, and southwest. The southwest quadrant of Houston consistently registered the largest number of housing discrimination complaints in the city. The western half of the city accounted for nearly two-thirds of the complaints filed between 1979 and 1982. This high level of complaint activity in Houston's northwest and southwest quadrants relative to the east side reflects the rapid development of these areas. Southwest Houston, for example, accounted for a large share of the new development in the city, especially in multifamily housing. This quadrant of the city accounts for nearly 50 percent of Houston's multifamily housing units.

A comprehensive study of housing discrimination in Houston was conducted in 1980.[20] The data for this study included one hundred randomly selected complaints filed with the city's Fair Housing Division between 1975 and 1978. A demographic profile of the study sample revealed that 67 percent of the subjects were female and 43 percent male; more than three-fourths (77 percent) of the complaint sample came from black, Hispanic, or Oriental households.[21] The largest number of complaints (nearly two-thirds) filed with the Fair Housing Division charged discrimination based on race; sex discrimination was the second most frequent type of complaint, constituting a little more than one-fifth of the total number of complaints. One in ten complaints alleged discrimination based on national origin.

The geographic origin of housing discrimination in Houston was related to several demographic factors. For example, neighborhood ethnic composition and increases in the proportion of housing units that were multifamily were related to the level of complaint activity. More than 41 percent of the housing discrimination complaints originated in census tracts that had less than 10 percent minority population. The overall complaint activity decreased as the percentage of minority group members increased in the census tract of the complaint. This pattern held up for all types of discrimination covered by the city's Fair Housing Ordinance, with the exception of sex discrimination, complaints of which originated about equally from minority and white neighborhoods. Minority females often bear the burden of being the victims of both sex and racial discrimination. A third factor, which could be termed "family life cycle," often compounds the burden of discrimination against minority women with children. In such cases, it is a safe maneuver for rental agents to refuse housing to a minority female with children because refusal to rent based on "life cycle" (i.e., having children) is not against the law.

Inasmuch as housing construction in Houston is not uniformly distributed throughout the city, the issue of mobility (the ability to exit one area and move into an area of one's choice) takes on added significance. The data in Table 5.2 give the location of housing discrimination com-

Table 5.2. Number of Complaints Filed, 1975–78, by Neighborhood Composition and Percent Change in Number of Multifamily Housing Units.

| | Number of Complaints | | |
| | *Percent Change in No. Multifamily Housing Units* | | |
Neighborhood Composition, 1970 (Percent Minority)	*Decrease*	*Low to Moderate Increase (0–29%)*	*Large Increase (30% or more)*
Less than 10	0 (0%)	16 (39%)	25 (61%)
10–40	5 (13%)	15 (45%)	20 (50%)
41+	4 (21%)	9 (47%)	6 (32%)
Total	9 (9%)	40 (40%)	51 (51%)

plaints by ethnic composition of the area and the change in the amount of multifamily housing. Over one-half of the discrimination complaints were from rapidly growing areas, that is, census tracts where multifamily housing stock grew at a rate of 30 percent or more. The boom in multifamily housing construction was also related to neighborhood composition; the most housing construction occurred in areas where there were few minorities, areas such as southwest Houston. These data support the idea that housing discrimination complaint activity is more frequent in high-growth areas and in neighborhoods that did not have a history of racially integrated housing.

Minority householders who are in the renter market have the general option of leasing housing in minority areas of the inner city or venturing out to the suburbs where housing availability is greater. However, black families who relocate outside minority areas often find insensitive and bigoted apartment managers who have "hidden" rental policies for minority households—more rigorous credit checks, unusually large security and rent deposits, or "ghettoization" (the steering of minority tenants to specific units within developments). For minorities, these barriers add to an already difficult problem of finding and securing decent and affordable housing for their family.

Minority areas within central cities are becoming more racially identifiable than they were a decade ago. Areas which are undergoing rapid growth and renewal are faced with the task of dismantling institutionalized discriminatory practices before they spread to new development areas. Houston is a classic example of this process. The Fair Housing Division was given the charge of assuring all Houstonians of equal access to the housing market. However, since many of the attitudes and practices of landlords, realtors, developers, and lending institutions evolved over several generations, the elimination of such practices and policies will not be an easy task. Discrimination has reached a level of sophistication that makes it easy to practice and difficult (if not impossible) to prove in a legal sense. Advertisements for racially segregated housing—"Whites Only"—are very rare. However, the hidden or informal occupancy preferences discussed earlier often achieve similar, if not the same, results as the more overt forms of housing discrimination.

Finally, blacks and other minority families can expect less enforcement of laws against housing discrimination than they did in the 1970s. Despite the numerous indications that housing discrimination remains a problem for minority families and families with children, federal enforcement agency staff (in the Justice Department, Civil Rights Commission, and so on) have had their budgets slashed. The dismantling of fair housing agencies on the local level, like Houston's, and the dismissal of their mission diminishes the housing options available to blacks and other minority households. However, the issues related to decent and affordable housing of one's choice continue to be a high-priority item on the black community's agenda.

6.

Environmental Quality and Houston's Neighborhoods

The environmental movement in the United States historically has been associated with the more educated upper class. However, many of the areas threatened by pollution and other forms of environmental degradation are found in or near lower-income, working-class, and minority neighborhoods. In a sense, those individuals and communities with proximity to health-threatening externalities—various forms of pollution, congestion, toxic wastes, and other hazards—are the real endangered species. Various networks and organizations have been formed over the years to redress the grievances that may result from the interplay between population, technology and the environment. Local governing bodies and citizens' groups often come to the realization that some form of regulation is required in the urban complex to preserve a balanced ecosystem.

Minority and lower-income neighborhoods often occupy the "wrong side of the tracks" and consequently may receive different treatment when it comes to enforcement of environmental regulations. The distinct groupings that emerge in urban areas are a result of "the distribution of wealth, patterns of racial and economic discrimination, access to jobs, housing, and a host of other variables."[1] Political and economic power are key factors which influence the spatial distribution of residential amenities or disamenities and often determine "who gets what, where, and how."[2]

The differential in the quality of life in affluent and poor neighborhoods has been clearly documented.[3] Pollution of all types takes a heavy toll on inner-city neighborhoods as a result of the high concentration of industry and the freeway systems that often crisscross lower-income and minority neighborhoods.[4] Middle- and upper-class residents have been more successful in changing the course of planned freeways than their lower-income counterparts, and air pollution from automobile exhaust can be found at levels up to five times greater in inner cities than in suburban areas. Middle- and upper-class households have the option of shutting out the fumes and odors with air conditioning. Older, inner-city areas frequently also have polluted water. Corroded water mains that are neither repaired nor replaced allow contaminants to seep into the water supply. Tap water in the lower-income inner-city areas often comes out rust-colored, with a definite odor and bearing sediments. Residents' tight budgets preclude the purchase of bottled drinking water or water purification devices.[5] They are forced by economic necessity to go without such luxuries and to adapt to lower-quality physical environments.

While the lower and working classes and minorities are subjected to a disproportionately large amount of pollution in the workplace, as well as in their neighborhoods, these groups have been only marginally involved in the nation's environmental movement.[6] The day-to-day lives of poor inner-city blacks, for example, differed greatly from those of the well-publicized environmentalists, who championed such large issues as wilderness and wildlife preservation, resource conservation, world population control, and industrial pollution abatement. Many of the battles which mainstream environmental organizations waged during the height of the movement in the early seventies had marginal effect on or relation to deteriorating conditions in central cities and had very little to do with the plight of blacks or the poor. Blacks were actively involved in civil rights struggles during the peak of the environmental movement. Many inner-city residents were engaged in a constant battle with problems they faced head-on every day: spiraling crime rates, drug trafficking, deteriorating infrastructures, housing and employment discrimination, high unemployment, widespread poverty, and a host of other urban ills which threatened their survival.

Persons who have mobility are less vulnerable to environmental problems than are the less mobile. People and businesses than can afford to flee to the suburbs do so, while the poor and less advantaged stay behind and suffer from poverty and pollution.[7] Institutional barriers (employment and housing discrimination; redlining by banks, mortgage companies, and insurance firms; public policies which tend to favor the affluent over the poor; and disparate enforcement of land-use and environmental regulations) relegate a large segment of urban residents to less than desirable physical environments, reduce housing and residential options, limit mobility, and increase risks from exposure to potentially health-threatening toxic material.[8] While environmental activism may have been dominated by persons with above average education, "concern about pollution is not the sole property of the suburban middle-class."[9] Minorities, lower-income, and working-class residents are also concerned about their physical environment.

LAND USE AND NEIGHBORHOOD QUALITY

Discharges of pollutants into the air and water, noise, vibrations, and aesthetic disamenities are often segregated from residential areas because of "public goods" or, more commonly, "public bads."[10] These disamenities are usually located in a particular area because their adverse effects generally fall off with distance from the source. Land-use zoning is commonly used as a "protectionist device" to ensure "a place for everything and everything in its place."[11] Zoning is ultimately intended to influence land use in accordance with long-range local needs or the community's comprehensive plan. Zoning is designed to segregate "lower" types of land use (industry, commerce and apartments) and their ill effects from the "highest" type of land use (single-family homes).[12] It is also worth noting that spatial organization, positions of urban social structure, and the distribution of land use all have a political dimension. Communities often compete for what they regard as more advantageous land use.[13]

Houston, however, has clung to its unique position of being the only major U.S. city without zoning. The 1970s saw the city's population grow by more than 362,000; the additional population exacerbated the already growing problems with traffic, pollution, and crowding. Numerous attempts have been made over the years to institute zoning to control land use and plan Houston's growth in an orderly fashion. All attempts have failed, however; for example, Houstonians in 1948 went to the poll and defeated zoning by a 2-to-1 margin.[14] A commission on zoning was established in 1959; in 1962 it completed work on a comprehensive plan that would zone the city into eleven residential, apartment, commercial, and manufacturing categories.[15] The zoning issue was soundly defeated in 1962 by 57 percent of the vote cast in a straw election. The greatest support for zoning came from upper-income residential areas and the greatest anti-zoning sentiment was registered by lower-income black neighborhoods. Zoning was seen as an exclusionary mechanism that would maintain residential segregation along racial and economic lines.

Houston's no-zoning policy has allowed the "scattering of offices and businesses in disarray over the landscape . . . and has created a burden of law enforcement with taverns located 'willy-nilly' through the city." [16] In the absence of zoning, independent developers have used renewable deed restrictions as a means of land-use control or regulation within their new subdivisions, although the city may become involved by passing injunctions or granting damages, through the courts, to claimants. It appears that variable enforcement and renewal of deed restrictions by area residents have figured largely into the regulation (or segregation) of undesirable externalities. [17] Specifically, lower-income and older neighborhoods tend to have difficulty enforcing and renewing deed restrictions; deed restrictions in these areas are often allowed to lapse, as the residents of these neighborhoods may be preoccupied with making a living and may not have the time, energy, or faith in the system to get the needed signatures to keep their deed restrictions in force. Moreover, the high occupancy turnover and large renter population in many inner-city and lower-income neighborhoods further weaken the efficacy of deed restrictions in regulating land use within these areas.

While the no-zoning attitude may be the prevailing view at Houston's city hall and among developers, there is mounting evidence that unrestrained growth has met its end. Beginning in the early eighties, the city council passed ordinances to restrict and/or regulate development activities. [18] For example, in 1982 the city enacted an ordinance which for the first time allowed it to control development activities in large, undivided tracts of land outside the central business district. This ordinance also established setback requirements for new buildings, that is, there had to be a certain distance between new buildings and major thoroughfares. [19] The city has enacted ordinances to regulate adult bookstores and "sex shops," billboards and signs, sewer line installations, building in flood-prone areas, junk and salvage yards, municipal landfills, and hazardous waste transportation and disposal. The city council, with backing from the Houston Chamber of Commerce, in 1986 took a serious step in the direction of zoning when it adopted the drafting of a comprehensive plan for Houston and its extraterritorial jurisdiction. The measure passed by a 10-to-2 margin. The Houston Board of Realtors, a major critic of the plan, labeled the decision a back-door move to zoning. [20]

In an effort to assess the efficacy of land-use controls and regulations already in effect in Houston's neighborhoods, the Houston Environmental Survey 83 was undertaken at Texas Southern University. [21] Data included in this study were derived from a 20-percent random sample of local neighborhood civic club presidents selected from 520 civic clubs found in the *1982 Directory of Houston Area Civic Organizations,* which was compiled by the mayor's Citizen Assistance Office. Only neighborhood civic clubs that fell within Houston's nine single-member council districts were used in the analysis. A total of 102 civic club presidents responded to the 104 questionnaires mailed, thus providing a response rate of 98 percent.

A demographic profile of the 102 civic club presidents surveyed revealed that nearly two-thirds (63.7 percent) were male. The ethnic composition of the study group showed that whites made up 60.7 percent, blacks 31.4 percent, Hispanics 6.9 percent, and other minorities 1.0 percent. Thus, 4 of every 10 civic club leaders surveyed could be classified as an ethnic minority. Blacks and Hispanics in 1980 made up 45 percent of Houston's population. The apparent underrepresentation of Hispanics as civic club presidents in the city is probably due to their more dispersed residential pattern (when compared with black housing patterns). Houston's black population is more residentially segregated than is the Hispanic population, and this makes it easier to elect a black civic club president.

A majority of the civic club leaders had completed college (65.7 percent); more than 83 percent of the subjects were employed in white-collar occupations; one-fifth (22.6 percent) were under the age of thirty-five, about one-half (48 percent) were between the ages of thirty-five and forty-nine, and more than one-fourth (29.4 percent) were age fifty or older. Nearly one-third (30.4 percent) were born in Houston; nearly one-half (48 percent) were not born in Houston but had lived there more than ten years; and one-fifth (21.6 percent) had lived in Houston less than ten years. Finally, respondents in the survey came from the following Houston quadrants: northeast (16.7 percent), northwest (22.5 percent), southeast (24.5 percent), and southwest (36.3 percent).

The major thrust of the environmental survey was to get the views of local civic leaders on land-use regulations and externalities that affect their respective neighborhoods as well as the city at large. More than eight of every ten (87.3 percent) civic club leaders surveyed expressed the opinion that Houston's growth had not been adequately planned. A by product of this unplanned and unrestrained growth appears to be an erosion of the quality of life in the city's residential areas.

There is little doubt that the pro-zoning sentiment is the prevailing view among civic club leaders. Zoning was supported by nearly two-thirds (64.7 percent) of the civic club leaders surveyed. This strong pro-zoning sentiment was exhibited across racial and class lines. However, the strongest endorsement of zoning came from the minority civic club presidents; more than three-fourths (76.3 percent) of this group sup-ported zoning for Houston. These findings contradict the results ob-tained in the city's straw vote of the early sixties, when black neighbor-hoods exhibited the least support for zoning. John Mixon, a University of Houston professor of law, boldly predicted in 1983 that Houston would have zoning within ten years. Mixon based his predictions on the changing political climate and on new inner-city development patterns. He stated that "residents of River Oaks, Southgate, Southhampton, and Tanglewood are getting tired of people in high-rise towers staring down into their back yards." [22]

Upper-income white neighborhoods such as those mentioned above and their residents are not alone in their frustration over the lack of a legal structure for redressing commercial expansion into residential areas. Similar feelings are shared in Houston's black and Hispanic neigh-borhoods. Instead of high-rise office buildings, however, the black com-munity has had to contend with garbage dumps, landfills, salvage yards, garages, sex shops, and a host of other nonresidential activities which threaten the stability of their neighborhoods.

The efficacy of deed restrictions in regulating land was called into question by the civic club leaders; less than one-half (43.2 percent) of the community leaders felt that deed restrictions had been effective in regulating land use in Houston. However, nearly three-fourths (72.5 per-

Table 6.1. Evaluations of Deed Restrictions by Location of Civic Club Leaders, 1983.

	Percent Agreeing with Statement[a]			
Statement	*Northeast* (N = 17)[b]	*Northwest* (N = 23)	*Southeast* (N = 25)	*Southwest* (N = 37)
Deed restrictions have been an effective means of regulating land use in Houston	35.3	30.4	48.0	48.6
Deed restrictions are rigidly en-forced in my neighborhood	31.3	43.5	43.5	59.5
Deed restrictions have been an effective means of regulating land use in my neighborhood	43.8	91.3	72.0	77.8

[a]The responses to the above items include the combined categories of "Agree" and "Strongly Agree."
[b]N = number of respondents.

Table 6.2. Evaluations of Deed Restrictions by Race of Civic Club Leaders, 1983.

	Percent Agreeing with Statement[a]	
Statement	*White* (N = 62)[b]	*Nonwhite* (N = 40)
Deed restrictions have been an effective means of regulating land use in Houston	46.8	35.0
Deed restrictions are rigidly enforced in my neighborhood	54.1	36.8
Deed restrictions have been an effective means of regulating land use in my neighborhood	83.3	60.0

[a] The responses to the above items include the combined categories of "Agree" and "Strongly Agree."
[b] N = number of respondents.

cent) of the respondents indicated that deed restrictions were effective only at the neighborhood level. Neighborhood deed restrictions were considered to be most effective in northwest and southwest Houston neighborhoods, that is, in the more recently developed subdivisions. The evaluations of deed-restriction enforcement also varied with neighborhood location (see Table 6.1). Specifically, less than one-third of the northeast civic club leaders felt that deed restrictions were rigidly enforced in their neighborhoods, while more than one-half of the leaders from the southwest gave a similar response; deed-restriction enforcement was rated the same by representatives from northwest and southeast neighborhoods.

Minority group civic leaders tended to have less confidence in the efficacy of deed restrictions as neighborhood controls than did white civic leaders (see Table 6.2). More than 54 percent of the whites but only 37 percent of the minority leaders felt that deed restrictions were rigidly enforced in their respective neighborhoods. This disparity may be because blacks and Hispanics often reside in older neighborhoods, with low owner-occupancy rates and a large share of the city's lower-income inhabitants. The city is often negligent in its enforcement of deed restrictions and ordinances in minority neighborhoods, and voluntary compliance is harder to obtain in this lax atmosphere. Neighborhoods with a high proportion of homeowners (white or black), however, are more successful in getting compliance on restrictions, in gaining the support of a city council member, and so on. The problem is that a black neighborhood of homeowners may be surrounded by or adjacent to lower-income areas—with renters and absentee landlords. The interests of the latter run counter to those of homeowners; landlords make more money on multifamily housing and will convert available single-family homes to, for example, fourplexes, often with violations of fire and other safety codes. Prosecuting these slumlords would result in the removal of low-cost housing from the market, leaving the low-income tenants homeless. Thus, the landlords have little to fear from the city or civic associations; this situation produces an "anything goes" attitude and leads to the physical decline of a neighborhood.

The major city-wide environmental problems, as reported by civic club leaders, included solid waste, water pollution, and air pollution. Over one-half (54 percent) of the civic club leaders indicated that the city's management of waste, which included litter, trash, and solid waste, was a "very serious" problem; 45 percent of the civic leaders felt that air pollution was a "very serious" problem in the city.

Community leaders' views on environmental quality varied with neighborhood location (see Table 6.3). Civic club leaders from northeast Houston, for example, tended to rate nearly every item on environmental quality in their neighborhood as much more severe than did respondents from other sectors of the city. Air and water pollution and neighborhood encroachment by business and industry were considered to be major problems by more than three-fourths of the civic club leaders from the northeast Houston neighborhoods. Much of the city's heavy

Table 6.3. Neighborhood Concerns by Location of Civic Club Leaders, 1983.

Environmental Problem	Percent Respondents Indicating "Severe Problem"[a]			
	Northeast (N = 17)[b]	Northwest (N = 23)	Southeast (N = 25)	Southwest (N = 37)
Water pollution	75.6	30.4	28.0	38.9
Air pollution	82.4	43.5	48.0	37.8
Noise	52.9	34.7	28.0	30.6
Litter, trash, and solid waste	53.0	34.8	44.0	59.4
Overcrowded residential areas	41.2	21.7	4.0	5.4
Overcrowded recreation facilities	53.0	52.1	52.0	29.7
Commercial expansion into residential areas	76.4	43.4	40.0	59.4
Industrial expansion into residential area	82.3	26.1	16.0	32.4

[a] The responses include the combined categories of "Somewhat Severe" and "Very Severe" problems in the neighborhood location.
[b] N = number of respondents.

industry is concentrated in the northeast quadrant; the mostly black working-class neighborhoods in this sector have endured the increasing expansion of industry into their area since the early sixties.

Crowding of recreational facilities and air pollution were cited as major problems by nearly one-half of the civic club leaders from the northwest and southwest quadrants of the city. Representatives from southwest Houston neighborhoods cited litter, trash, solid waste, and commercial expansion into their residential areas as major concerns. The heavily populated southwest quadrant of the city has placed an extreme hardship on Houston's solid waste department. It appears that civic club presidents who represent southwest Houston neighborhoods continue to voice concern about the city's garbage problem. Moreover, the area's rapid increase in multifamily housing attracted an equally large number of commercial enterprises and high-rise office buildings. No doubt persons whose homes and neighborhoods lay in the path of this expansion felt threatened.

Community attitudes toward pollution have been found to be influenced by (1) the psychological makeup of residents, (2) social characteristics of the residents, and (3) the actual levels of pollution.[23] The assessment of government's and industry's roles in promoting and preserving a safe environment is influenced by neighborhood location and ethnicity of the neighborhood.

The data in Table 6.4 reveal that civic club presidents who represent neighborhoods in the eastern half of Houston were more likely to be critical of government and industry efforts to control pollution than were their counterparts in the western half of the city. Civic club presidents from the east side were also more likely than their counterparts on the west side to endorse the idea that "jobs are more important than the environment." This apparent paradox can be explained in part by the high degree of economic dependence on nearby industries by many working-class residents on the city's east side. Minority group members, who often live in polluted environments, expressed a strong sense of mistrust regarding the responsibility of government and industry in environmental reform. On the other hand, minority community leaders were more than twice as likely as their white counterparts to rank jobs above the environment in importance; more than 45 percent of the minority civic club presidents agreed that "jobs are more important than the environment," with only 21 percent of the whites expressing a similar view (see Table 6.5).

Table 6.4. Civic Club Leaders' Support for Environmental Reform by Houston Location, 1983.

	Percent Agreeing with Statement[a]			
Statement	*Northeast* (N = 17)[b]	*Northwest* (N = 23)	*Southeast* (N = 25)	*Southwest* (N = 37)
More government effort is needed to control pollution	88.2	78.2	84.0	72.9
Industry should be allowed to handle pollution in its own way	17.7	4.3	12.0	18.9
Pollution laws have become too strict in recent years	17.6	17.3	4.0	27.0
Industry is dragging its feet in cleaning up the environment	88.3	65.2	84.0	59.4
Jobs are more important than the environment	52.5	17.3	32.0	27.0

[a]This category represents the combined responses of "Strongly Agree" and "Mildly Agree" on the scale.
[b]N = number of respondents.

Table 6.5. Support for Environmental Reform by Race of Civic Club Leaders.

	Percent Agreeing with Statements[a]	
Statement	*White* (N = 62)[b]	*Nonwhite* (N = 40)
More government effort is needed to control pollution	74.1	87.5
Industry should be allowed to handle pollution in its own way	11.3	17.5
Pollution laws have become too strict in recent years	20.9	12.5
Industry is dragging its feet in cleaning up the environment	59.7	90.0
Jobs are more important than the environment	20.9	45.0

[a]This category represents the combined responses of "Strongly Agree" and "Mildly Agree" on the scale.
[b]N = number of respondents.

The land-use patterns that have evolved in Houston over the years in the absence of zoning are now being challenged at the grass-roots level and at city hall. Redevelopment activities within Houston's inner city, along with the changing political climate, have contributed to lower-income and minority neighborhood residents' dissatisfaction with deed restrictions as the chief form of land-use control. Broad-based support exists for supplementing the city's deed restrictions and ordinances with some form of zoning.

THE CITY'S DUMPING GROUNDS

Public officials learn fast that solid waste management is often a volatile political issue. Controversy centers around charges that disposal sites are not equitably distributed among the different quadrants of a city, which would spread the burden more equitably and lessen public opposition.[24] Nowhere is this more apparent than in Houston. Discriminatory public policy decisions, unequal growth within the city, the absence of effective land-use regulations, and residential segregation are all important factors contributing to wide differences in physical environments in the Houston area.[25]

Public awareness has increased in recent years on the issues of pollution and the possible health risks that may surround waste disposal. Although the American public's level of awareness has been raised, the drama surrounding the discovery of "inactive" toxic waste sites has eclipsed the controversy surrounding the selection of disposal sites for urban garbage and solid waste.[26] Municipal landfills do pose a potential health threat. For example, sanitary landfills and city sewer systems are "a favorite point of discharge for toxic chemicals hauled by moonlight disposers."[27] A 1983 report to Congress by the Office of Technology Assessment revealed that the United States is generating more than 250 million metric tons of hazardous waste each year, or about one metric ton (2,205 pounds) per U.S. citizen.[28] Current regulations cover only approximately 40 million tons of this massive amount of waste, while millions of tons of this unregulated and potentially harmful waste simply go to sanitary landfills designed for municipal garbage. There is a general consensus among leading experts that sanitary landfills receiving such wastes will likely leak toxic substances into the environment.[29]

Finding suitable sites for sanitary landfills is a critical problem mainly because people are reluctant to live near a facility where garbage is legally dumped and where toxic materials may be illegally dumped. The standard public reaction to landfill site selection has been the NIMBY principle—"Not in My Back Yard." But Houston city officials in the pre-1970s era seemed to reflect a PIBBY principle—"Place in Blacks' Back Yard." Since the 1930s the city has used basically two methods of disposing of its solid waste: incineration and landfilling.[30]

Table 6.6. City of Houston Garbage Incinerators and Municipal Landfills.

Neighborhood	Location	Incin-erator	Landfill	Target Area[a]	Ethnicity of Neigh-borhood[b]
Fourth Ward	Southwest	1	1	Yes	Black
Cottage Grove	Northwest	1	—	Yes	Black
Kashmere Gardens	Northeast	2	—	Yes	Black
Sunnyside	Southeast	1	2	Yes	Black
Navigation	Southeast	1	—	Yes	Hispanic
Larchmont	Southwest	1	—	No	White
Carverdale	Northwest	1	—	Yes	Black
Trinity Gardens	Northeast	—	1	Yes	Black
Acres Homes	Northwest	—	1	Yes	Black

[a] Target areas are designated neighborhoods under Houston's Community Development Block Grant program, which is funded by HUD and administered by the city, designed to upgrade housing, streets, infrastructures, health and human services, and employment in low-income neighborhoods.
[b] Ethnicity of neighborhood represents the racial/ethnic group which constitutes a numerical majority in the census tracts that make up the neighborhood.

The data in Table 6.6 show the location of the city-owned waste disposal facilities. A total of thirteen disposal facilities were operated by the city from the late twenties to the mid-seventies.

The siting policies of municipalities and private disposal companies have contributed to black and lower-income communities becoming the dumping grounds for urban garbage and illegally dumped hazardous wastes.[31] The city operated eight garbage incinerators (five large-type units and three mini units). Six of them were located in black neighborhoods, one was in a Hispanic neighborhood, and the eighth site was in a predominantly white area. All five of the large incinerators were located in minority neighborhoods. Four were in black neighborhoods (Fourth Ward, West End–Cottage Grove, Kashmere Gardens, and Sunnyside). The fifth large incinerator operated in the Segundo Barrio, or Second Ward, the mostly Hispanic Navigation Road area.

The cost of operating these large units and the pollution generated by these systems were major factors in their closing (the last one closed in 1972). The city contracted with a private company, Houston Natural Gas, to conduct a pilot project in which mini-incinerators would be used. These were supposed to be more efficient, cost less to operate, and generate less pollution. The City of Houston in 1972 invested $1.9 million in a contractual agreement with Houston Natural Gas for three of the "pollution-free" mini-incinerators. One of them was located on Westpark near the Larchmont and Sharpstown neighborhoods, another site was on Kelly Street in the Kashmere Gardens neighborhood, and the third site was located on Sommermeyer Street in the Carverdale neighborhood. Larchmont and Sharpstown are mostly white areas, while Kashmere Gardens and Carverdale are predominantly black neighborhoods. Pilot tests of the mini-incinerators found the claim of "pollution free" to be exaggerated. The units did not meet the pollution standards of the Houston Air Quality Control Board and were shut down in the mid-seventies after a short period of operation.

The city operated five municipal landfills variously from the 1920s through the 1970s. All five of these landfills were located in black neighborhoods.[32] Jefferson Davis Hospital, a charity hospital that is part of the Harris County Hospital District, sits on top of the old Fourth Ward garbage dump. This dump site once extended from Taft Street, on the west, all the way to Lamb Street, on the east. Unlike all the other municipal landfills in Houston, the one in the Fourth Ward was reclaimed, and the hospital was constructed there in 1937–38. The other four municipal landfills have remained and are unfortunately just about the only "hills" in the flat Houston landscape. When one drives south on Almeda Road or the South Freeway (State Highway 288), the old city landfill mounds in Sunnyside and the mounds of the Holmes Road landfills near Almeda Plaza dominate the landscape. This situation can also be seen in northeast Houston if one drives east on Little York Road toward Mesa Drive. The Whispering Pines landfill dominates the landscape just east of the Northwood Manor subdivision, a mostly black neighborhood where more than 88 percent of the residents owned their homes in 1980. It is no wonder that neighborhood residents who live near these landfills have dubbed the mounds "mount trashmores."

The Sunnyside neighborhood had two city-owned municipal landfills. The Sunnyside landfill proper dates back to the fifties, and adjacent to this site is the Reed Road landfill. These two sites are located just east of the old Holmes Road incinerator. These facilities all lie in the heart of an all-black neighborhood with a long and rich history as a semirural black community. Sunnyside developed as a self-contained, segregated community in the 1940s, and much of the development of the neighborhood took place along Holmes Road. The major business corridor was along Reed Road, which historically is to Sunnyside what Lyons Avenue is to the Fifth Ward, Dowling Street is to the Third Ward, and West Dallas Street is to the Fourth Ward.

The Kirkpatrick landfill in the predominantly black Trinity Gardens neighborhood operated during 1970 and 1971. Residents strongly protested the operation of the landfill in their neighborhood; they organized marches and demonstrations and attempted to block city garbage trucks from dumping at the site. The newly elected black city councilman—the first black to sit on the Houston City Council—Judson Robinson, Jr., intervened to quell the near-riot conditions. However, the site was opened but operated for only a short period of time as a concession to residents, although the city was already planning to get out of the landfill business altogether and turn it over to the private sector.

The old West Donovan landfill site off Ella Boulevard is often referred to as the Acres Homes dump. Acres Homes is a mostly black neighborhood in the mostly white northwestern quadrant of the city, and there is a long history of uncontrolled dump sites operating in the neighborhood. The landscape there is replete with illegally dumped material along the roadways, in the heavily wooded areas, and at the now-closed city-owned landfill site. The problem of illegal dumping is not confined to Acres Homes, but it is an acute problem in all areas near landfills. This is true for sites that have been filled or closed and for those still in operation.

The perception of "once a landfill always a landfill" is one contributing factor to the illegal dumping. Another factor is that the cost of legally dumping waste material at landfills is more than many people are willing to pay. The city council in 1985 attempted to curtail the illegal dumping by setting up neighborhood waste drop-off sites in several lower-income neighborhoods. These sites serve as temporary holding stations for waste material (excluding household garbage) dropped off by area residents. Commercial haulers are excluded from this program; the service is free to residents of the area. The waste material is later taken to the landfill for permanent disposal. The program has provided lower-income residents with an alternative to the high landfill fees charged for dumping, but it has not curtailed the illegal dumping by small private haulers, the so-called "midnight" dumpers, who leave their loads in lower-income areas as a way of getting around the fees charged for legally disposing of waste at the landfills.

Although blacks constituted a little more than one-fourth of Houston's population, black neighborhoods housed three-fourths of the city-owned solid waste disposal facilities. Lower-income areas contain twelve of the thirteen city-owned solid waste disposal sites, which are located in designated Community Development Block Grant (CDBG) program target areas, selected according to poverty level, housing quality, crowding, and minority concentration. (The federally funded program provides job-training, home repair loans, street repair and health services in multi-purpose centers.) Houston has twenty-five of these CDBG target areas, of which eight had city-owned waste disposal facilities. Lower-income black neighborhoods have truly become the dumping grounds for the rest of the city's garbage.

The Texas Department of Health is the state agency that grants permits for standard sanitary landfills, or Type I landfills. Type I landfill sites are "required in a county having a population of 100,000 or more or for sites serving 5,000 persons or more." [33] The Texas Department of Health during the 1970–78 period issued permits for a total of four standard sanitary landfills for Houston. The figures in Table 6.7 illustrate that siting of privately owned sanitary landfills for the disposal of Houston's solid waste. The figures in Table 6.7 illustrate that the siting of privately owned sanitary landfills generally followed the pattern established by the city government: private disposal sites too are likely to be placed in predominantly black neighborhoods. Three of the four privately owned landfill sites which receive Houston's solid waste are located in predominantly black Almeda Plaza and Northwood Manor. The fourth site is located in a sparsely populated industrial area south of the mostly white Chattwood subdivision.

The Whispering Pines landfill was the subject of a hard-fought legal battle. In 1979 residents from the Northwood Manor subdivision filed a lawsuit in federal court to stop the construction of the landfill in their neighborhood. The black residents and their attorney charged the Texas Department of Health and a private disposal company with old-fashioned racial discrimination in the selection of the Whispering Pines landfill site. [34] Residents were upset because not only was the site near their homes, it was only 1,400 feet from the neighborhood high school,

Table 6.7. Privately Owned Houston Sanitary Landfills Issued Permits by the Texas Department of Health, 1970–78.

Landfill Site	Location	Year Permitted	Neighborhood	Ethnicity of Neighborhood
Holmes Road	Southeast	1970	Almeda Plaza	Black
McCarty	Northeast	1971	Chattwood [a]	White
Holmes Road	Southeast	1978	Almeda Plaza	Black
Whispering Pines	Northeast	1978	Northwood Manor	Black

[a] This predominantly white neighborhood is located just north of the McCarty landfill. The Chattwood neighborhood lies within Houston's Community Development Settegast Target Area, which has undergone a dramatic racial transition, from 40 percent black in 1970 to more than 70 percent black in 1980.

the M. D. Smiley High School Complex, as well as Jones-Cowart Stadium and athletic field, the North Forest Independent School District's general administration building, and the district's school bus facility. North Forest ISD is a suburban district in which more than 85 percent of the students are black (1980 enrollment figures). Seven North Forest ISD schools, which form a cluster, are located in the general area of the Whispering Pines landfill.

The judge ruled against the residents, and the landfill was built. The residents' suit, however, did produce some change. First, the Houston City Council, acting under intense pressure from the residents of Northwood Manor, passed a resolution in 1980 which prohibited city-owned solid waste trucks from dumping at the privately owned Whispering Pines landfill.[35] Second, the Texas Department of Health updated its requirements for landfill permits so that applicants had to include detailed land-use, economic, and sociodemographic data for areas near proposed Type I landfill sites. Third, and probably most important, blacks sent a clear signal to the Texas Department of Health, city government, and private waste disposal companies that they would fight any future attempts to place garbage dumps, landfills, and any other type of waste disposal facility in their neighborhoods.

The political implications of waste disposal siting and institutional discrimination have hampered the development of a comprehensive long-range disposal strategy for Houston's solid waste. Such a plan will need to distribute the burden of disposal if it is to get public acceptance. Since all residents produce waste, no one segment of the community should have to suffer the consequences of its disposal. In addition, innovative reclamation plans need to be developed which involve both the public and private sectors in resource recovery and recycling the inactive landfill sites that are scattered over the Houston landscape. Such reclamation plans need to be part of any future proposals for Type I landfill sites in the Houston area.

7.

Sharing the Economic Pie

A relatively low cost of living, combined with the potential for earning an above-average income, made Houston a desirable place in which to relocate during the seventies. As late as 1980, Houston had the twenty-third lowest cost of living of the twenty-five major metropolitan areas in the United States. In addition, the Houston SMSA was ranked fifteenth nationally in per capita income in 1978, a jump from seventy-sixth in 1969.[1]

The U.S. Department of Labor computes annual cost-of-living figures each year for forty U.S. cities. These cost-of-living figures are computed for a hypothetical urban family of four with one wage earner, a non-working spouse, and two children. The figures are broken down into three levels: lower, middle, and upper income. The 1977 annual cost of living in Houston for a lower-income family was $9,221; for a middle-income family, $15,488; and for an upper-income family, $22,421. Houston was ranked seventh lowest in cost-of-living averages among the forty cities surveyed.[2] Four years later, in 1981, the cost of living for a Houston family had increased to $14,810 for a lower-income family, $23,601 for a middle-income family, and $34,728 for an upper-income family.[3]

BLACKS IN THE LABOR FORCE

The Houston metropolitan area was a leading employment market in terms of jobs created during the seventies, with more than 669,700 new nonagricultural jobs added in this period. The Houston area produced more than 107,700 new jobs in 1978 (its peak year), 98,300 new jobs in

1979, and 59,700 new jobs in 1980. Finance, insurance, real estate, construction, services, and the trade industry were the major areas of this employment boom. It is estimated that nearly 41 percent of the new jobs projected for Houston through 1995 will be in the service occupations.[4] Growth appears to have occurred at a disproportionate rate in the professional, managerial, and clerical occupations. The Texas Employment Commission has estimated that the professional and managerial jobs will account for more than 32 percent of the net employment gains in the area; the clerical fields will account for nearly 25 percent of the employment gains up to 1995.[5]

Houston's strong economy during the seventies allowed it to expand despite major nationwide recessions during that decade. The unemployment rate in the Houston area remained significantly lower than the national average, even into the recession of the early eighties. For example, the 1981 unemployment rate for the Houston SMSA averaged around 4.6 percent, compared with 7.6 percent nationwide. Although the overall unemployment rate in the Houston metropolitan area was quite low in 1981, the black unemployment rate in the area was 7.5 percent (approximately twice the 3.8 percent unemployment rate for whites).[6] The Houston SMSA had a population in 1983 of more than 2.9 million persons, of whom 528,513 were black (18.2 percent of the metropolitan area's population).[7] More than 311,680 blacks worked in the Houston metropolitan area labor force in 1983, making their labor force participation rate 58.9 percent, as compared with a 64.7 percent for whites in the Houston area. The economic recession of the eighties contributed to a double-digit unemployment rate in black Houston (Table 7.1). The 1983 unemployment rate for the area's blacks was 15.5 percent, as compared with 9.1 percent for the Houston area. In January, 1986, 12.5 percent of blacks were unemployed in Houston, compared with 5.7 percent of whites.

The Houston area proved to be less than a worker's paradise for some

Table 7.1. Blacks in the Houston Area Labor Market, January, 1983.

	Population	Labor Force	Employed Workers	Unemployed Workers	Unemployment Rate
Total blacks	528,513	311,680	264,450	47,230	15.2
Black females	274,004	149,149	127,100	22,049	14.8
Black males	254,509	162,531	137,350	25,181	15.5

Source: TEC, "Labor Market Estimates: Affirmative Action Information," Houston District, January, 1983.

Houstonians. Local black workers not only have difficulty finding employment but also must contend with the "last hired, first fired" phenomenon that often becomes an active policy of employers during economic recessions. This policy is practiced in the private sector as well as at city hall. The task of devising employee layoff strategies during economic hard times is complicated by seniority systems and affirmative action plans. Layoffs based on a strict seniority system generally account for a larger number of blacks losing their jobs compared with other plans. However, because of institutionalized discrimination, seniority does not necessarily translate into job security for blacks. When the city laid off 770 employees in July, 1986, most of them were from the health, library, parks, and solid waste departments—at the lower end of the city's pay scale and heavily minority. Nearly 60 percent of those laid off were black. Whites constitute 47 percent of the city's work force, but only 18 percent of those laid off were white.

The racial distribution of Houston workers among the available jobs may be a contributing factor in the discrepancy between the unemployment rates of blacks and whites. For example, whites are more likely than blacks to be employed in white-collar occupations, where unemployment is generally lower than other occupational categories. The data in Table 7.2 show that nearly two-thirds (64.2 percent) of the whites in the Houston SMSA were employed in white-collar occupations, as compared with nearly two-fifths (39.1 percent) of the area's

Table 7.2. Employment by Occupation and Race in the Houston SMSA, 1980.

	(Percent)	
Occupational Category	*White*	*Black*
White-collar workers:		
Professional, technical, kindred	17.9	11.0
Managers and administrators, except farm	14.5	4.5
Sales workers	12.7	6.3
Clerical	19.1	17.3
Blue-collar workers:		
Craftsmen, kindred	15.5	11.1
Operative, including transport	8.9	19.3
Laborers, except farm	3.5	9.6
Service workers:		
Service workers, except household	6.9	17.6
Private household	0.2	2.4
Farmworkers	0.8	0.9
Total	100.0	100.0

Source: U.S. Bureau of the Census, 1980.

black workers. Whites were nearly three and one-half times as likely to be employed in managerial occupations as were blacks; whites were twice as likely to be employed in sales occupations as were blacks.

Black workers, on the other hand, are clustered in the blue-collar occupations. Two-fifths (40 percent) of the area's blacks worked in blue-collar occupations, whereas only a little more than one-fourth (27.9 percent) of the area's white workers were employed in blue-collar occupations. Blacks were more than three times as likely as their white counterparts to be employed in the service occupations; only 7 percent of the Houston area whites and 20 percent of the blacks worked in service occupations.

Blue-collar or manufacturing jobs have not fared well in the economic recessions of the eighties in Houston or across the nation. Oil glut–induced economic recessions forced Houston to join the rest of the nation in developing strategies to lessen the blow of economic hard times. Both public and private promotional campaigns have been initiated to attract new industry to the area and thereby diversify the local economy. These findings would lead one to speculate that persons who relocate to Houston without the technical skills or necessary educational background will likely find themselves in the growing unemployment lines with other Houston residents who have similar backgrounds. Many migrants to the Houston area discovered a city that was very competitive and politically conservative—not the expected utopia with unlimited opportunities for all. This received national publicity in 1983 in the form of "Tent City." Tent City was an all-white squatter settlement or shantytown under a bridge over the San Jacinto river where the unemployed and homeless ended up when "Boomtown" went bust.

THE INCOME GAP

An income gap between black and white families has always existed, although that gap narrowed somewhat during the early seventies. However, this trend began to reverse in the late seventies and early eighties (see Table 7.3). Nationally, the median income of black families in 1970 was $13,325 (in constant 1980 dollars) as compared with $21,722 for whites in the same year, or 61 percent of whites' income. By 1980 black median family income had dropped to less than 58 percent of the white median family's income.[8] Thus, black families actually lost purchasing power over this ten-year period.

Table 7.3. Median Income of Families Nationwide by Race, 1970–1980.

	(In Constant 1980 Dollars)		Ratio of Black to White
Year	Black	White	Income
1980	12,674	21,904	0.579
1979	13,219	23,275	0.568
1978	13,741	23,200	0.592
1977	13,004	22,763	0.571
1976	13,378	22,490	0.595
1975	13,441	21,845	0.615
1974	13,378	22,404	0.597
1973	13,479	22,354	0.603
1972	13,520	22,748	0.594
1971	13,103	21,714	0.603
1970	13,325	21,722	0.613

Source: U.S. Bureau of the Census, *Consumer Income*, Series P-60, No. 132, table 17, 1982.

Table 7.4. Median Family Income for Blacks and Whites in Selected Southern Metropolitan Areas, 1980.

	Median Family Income (Dollars)			Ratio of Black to White
SMSA	Total	Black	White	Income
Atlanta	21,409	13,903	23,630	58.8
Dallas–Fort Worth	21,869	13,675	23,602	57.9
Houston	23,959	16,069	26,439	60.8
Miami	18,756	13,802	20,205	68.3
New Orleans	19,028	11,798	21,944	61.8
San Antonio	17,473	12,526	18,642	67.2
Tampa–St. Petersburg	16,515	10,504	17,007	61.8

Source: U.S. Bureau of the Census, *Social, Economic and Housing Characteristics* (Washington, D.C.: Government Printing Office, 1982).

The median income of all American families was $19,908 in 1980. A number of large metropolitan areas in the South including the Houston, Dallas–Fort Worth, and Atlanta SMSAs had median family incomes above the national average (see Table 7.4). The $23,959 median family (all racial groups) income for the Houston SMSA in 1980 was higher than that of any other metropolitan area in the South. But even in once-prosperous Houston the income gap between black and white families has persisted. The average white family in the Houston metropolitan area earned $26,439 in 1980 as compared with $16,069 for the average black family.[9] The average black Houston family earned not quite 61 cents for every dollar earned by a white family in 1980.

Blacks in the Houston area earned higher incomes than did blacks in other metropolitan areas of the South. However, the discrepancy between black and white family incomes was smaller in the Miami, San Antonio, New Orleans, and Tampa–St. Petersburg metropolitan areas than in the Houston area. On the other hand, the black-white income gap of the Atlanta and Dallas–Fort Worth metropolitan areas was greater than that found in the Houston area. Overall, Houston's black community is the most affluent black community (as measured by 1980 median family income) in the South.

POVERTY AND THE POOR

Numerous federal programs were initiated in the 1960s and 1970s to improve the economic conditions of lower-income families in the nation, with mixed results. Poverty remains a way of life for about 12 percent of the country's families, that is, those across the poverty threshold ($9,287 for a family of four in 1980). Black families suffer disproportionately; they are more than three times as likely to be found in poverty as are white families. More than one-third of the nation's black families were below the poverty line in 1980, and that number increased in the eighties, particularly for female-headed households. The number of black female-headed households rose from 834,000 in 1970 to 1.4 million in 1981. These families accounted for 56 percent of all poor black families in 1970 and 70 percent in 1981.[10] These demographic changes are occurring at the same time that social and human resources programs for the poor are being cut or eliminated altogether.

The data in Table 7.5 show that 6.2 percent of whites in the Houston

Table 7.5. Poverty Levels in Selected Southern Metropolitan Areas.

SMSA	Total Black Population	Number below Poverty	Percent below Poverty (Black)	Percent below Poverty (White)
Atlanta	491,836	127,971	26.0	7.2
Dallas–Fort Worth	416,180	104,597	25.1	6.4
Houston	521,512	117,030	21.4	6.2
Miami	275,164	84,301	30.6	10.3
New Orleans	381,940	143,872	37.7	9.3
San Antonio	68,096	19,802	29.1	16.3
Tampa–St. Petersburg	141,785	49,713	35.1	9.4

Source: U.S. Bureau of the Census, *Social, Economic, and Housing Characteristics* (Washington, D.C.: Government Printing Office, 1982).

area fell below the poverty level, while more than 21.4 percent of the area's blacks were poor. Blacks in the Houston area were nearly three and one-half times (one in five) as likely to be found in poverty as were their white counterparts. The more than 117,030 poor blacks make up a sizable portion of the area's population.

Poverty exists as a social ill amid the sparkling glass and concrete towers of Houston and Dallas, as well as among the white sand and palm trees of Miami and Tampa. The problems which accompany urban poverty are not new. However, federal cutbacks have caused many local governing bodies to reduce services that were traditionally targeted toward the poor (housing subsidies, child care, job training for the hard-core unemployed, job programs for minority youth, health clinics, food stamps, hot meals for the elderly, hot lunches in the schools, financial aid for college-bound youth), thus worsening the already-deteriorating conditions of the nation's poor families. These conditions make it more difficult, if not impossible, for poor families to break the cycle of poverty. This point is highlighted by the fact that the percentage of black families below the poverty line was basically the same in 1980 as it was in 1970.

Houston's black poverty pockets are the invisible Houston, a city hidden within the well-publicized city of traffic and shopping centers. Efforts to ameliorate the problems of the poor in lower-income Houston neighborhoods, through such programs as Model Cities and Community Development Block Grants, have achieved mixed results. The Community Development Block Grant (CDBG) program was established under Title I of the Housing and Community Development Act of 1974 by the U.S. Congress, and the city of Houston became involved in the CDBG program in 1975. Houston received more than $251 million in CDBG during the period from 1975 to 1986. The local CDBG program, however, has had minimal effect in reversing the physical decline of the city's poverty pockets.

The federally funded local jobs program under the Comprehensive Employment and Training Act of 1973, or CETA, was another program designed to help Houston's hard-core unemployed and underemployed become full-time workers in better-paying, skilled occupations. Houston's CETA program was supposed to locate and process its clients, make them "job ready," provide skills and on-the-job training, locate jobs, and place its clients in jobs. The program had marginal, if any, effect on the wage scale and employment status of its participants. CETA participants often remained unemployed or in low-paying, dead-end jobs such as picking up litter and debris along roads, cutting grass, and other unskilled laborer positions. In many cases, the "trained" workers were no better off than prior to their training. Houston's CETA program was mired in controversy that often centered on the handling of funds, the selection of participants, and the cost-benefit of the federal manpower training program.

The problems that afflicted Houston's CETA program were present in a number of other cities. They were in fact so widespread that Congress, in 1983, enacted the Job Training Partnership Act as a replacement for CETA. Houston's CETA program was phased out in 1984, and the Houston Job Training and Partnership Council (HJTPC) program took its place. The HJTPC program emphasized privatization and voluntarism in creating a partnership between business and government. The program served twelve thousand individuals and placed more than five thousand participants in private-sector jobs in 1985. The HJPTC program exceeded its predicted job placement by 15 percent in 1985.[11]

Diminishing commitment to eliminating poverty has been manifested in budget cuts for social programs. These programs can be aggressively cut because the poor have few allies in decision-making positions. For example, the city's CDGB program for the years 1980–85 has seen a 29-percent reduction in funds. Reductions are also expected in the upcoming years. Congress funded the program through 1988; after that no one knows what federal support will be given to cities. Budget cuts within Houston's city government because of revenue shortfalls appeared likely to reduce needed services such as neighborhood clinics and capital improvement projects in lower-income areas.

EDUCATIONAL ATTAINMENT

The period between 1940 and 1980 was a time of dramatic change in the educational attainment of blacks. Specifically, the proportion of black Americans over age twenty-five who were high-school graduates was only 8 percent in 1940, but that figure had grown to 51 percent in 1980; comparable figures for whites show gains from 26 percent in 1940 to 71 percent in 1980. The percentage of black college graduates increased during this period from about 1.3 percent in 1940 to 8 percent in 1980; the proportion of whites who had completed college grew from 5 percent in 1940 to 18 percent in 1980.[12] For individuals aged twenty-five to thirty-four, the 1981 data reveal that 24 percent of the whites and 12 per-

Table 7.6. Educational Attainment of Persons Twenty-five Years or Older by Race, 1980.

| | *(In percent)* | | | |
| | Houston SMSA | | United States | |
Total Years of School Completed	White	Black	White	Black
Elementary (0–8 years)	12	23	16	27
High school (1–3 years)	15	20	13	21
High-school graduate (4 years)	30	31	38	31
Some college (1–3 years)	20	16	15	13
College graduate (4 or more years)	23	10	18	8

Sources: U.S. Bureau of the Census, *Social, Economic and Housing Characteristics* (Washington, D.C.: Government Printing Office, 1982); U.S. Bureau of the Census, "Population Profile of the United States: 1981," *Current Population Reports*, Series P-20, No. 374 (1982); John Reid, "Black America in the 1980s," *Population Bulletin* 37, no. 4 (December, 1982): 25.

cent of blacks in that age group had completed college.[13] Despite the significant gains made over the past four decades, the persistent racial gap is unarguably present.[14]

The 1980 census figures on the Houston SMSA and its central city (i.e., Houston proper) show that the number of college-educated citizens grew in the seventies. The 1980 U.S. Census data show that more than 28 percent of Houston's whites and nearly 12 percent of the city's blacks had completed college.[15] However, these figures in the Houston SMSA again show the continued educational discrepancy between blacks and whites. For example, more than 43 percent of the blacks in the Houston metropolitan area had not completed high school in 1980, as compared with 27 percent of the whites (see Table 7.6). The percentage of blacks and whites who had completed high school was practically the same (three in every ten persons). However, roughly one-fourth (23 percent) of the whites in the Houston SMSA had completed college, as compared with 10 percent of the blacks.

The percentage of white college graduates in the Houston metropolitan area is more than double that of blacks, a finding that is consistent with national figures. A slightly higher percentage of the area's black population has attended college (at least one year) than has the black population nationwide (26 percent of black Houston twenty-five years or older compared with 20.4 percent of blacks nationwide). Houston also has one of the largest numbers of college-educated blacks of any community in the South.

Black families and workers have not "made it" in Houston. Houston is not an island in the South, but exists within a larger social, economic, and political system. The major economic issues, concerns, and problems present in the nation are also found in Houston. As in other major urban areas, blacks in Houston must contend with the problems of getting employed, staying employed, and earning a decent living in an era of dwindling resources.

8.

Black Business Trends

Minority group members, particularly blacks, remain underrepresented as business owners. The business participation rate of minorities in the United States is only one-fifth that of whites.[1] Business ownership rates also differ among the various minority groups. The Minority Business Development Agency examined the number of minority business enterprises (MBEs) nationwide per 1,000 businesses and found a distribution of 9.2 for blacks, 19.5 for Hispanics, and 28.8 for Asians.[2] The reasons given for low black business formation include an inadequate number of black business role models[3] and perceptions about the social status of business owners.[4] Black business owners often direct their children into the professions—law, medicine, engineering, or dentistry—perceiving those roles to have greater prestige than that of a business owner. Without the transfer of a business from one generation to the next, black businesses pass from existence, and then a lack of general knowledge about business,[5] lack of available capital,[6] and business opportunity restrictions hinder the formation of new businesses to take the place of those that are dissolved after their owners retire or die.[7] Business opportunity restrictions, although officially outlawed in the 1960s, may still exist in the form of prejudice toward blacks. Social and political forces often influence which businesses receive a license, or bid materials, or a contract. Market information is often transmitted to business owners by supplier representatives, who have a network of regular contacts in the field. If these suppliers are reluctant to communicate with black businesses, the vital information needed to compete will be reserved for white businesses. .

Black-owned firms tend to be located in areas with high concentrations of blacks; twenty-two states accounted for more than 84 percent of the black and other minority-owned business firms and 83 percent of the minority population.[8] The South had more than 50 percent of the black-owned businesses in 1980; more than 115,829 black businesses were located in the South, and these had gross receipts in excess of $3.5 billion.

CAPITALISM AND THE BLACK COMMUNITY

Black-owned firms continue to be a relatively small part of the United States' gross national product (GNP). In 1972 black business receipts accounted for 0.46 percent of the GNP, and this figure had dropped to 0.41 percent in 1982. Bourdon et al. assert that "black-owned firms will not maintain their position relative to the U.S. economy as a whole in the 1980's."[9] Andrew Brimmer, a noted economist, predicted in 1982 that blacks would likely expand their share of the total U.S. business receipts in the 1980s but would continue to lose black customers to white firms. Brimmer writes: "Black firms accounted for $11.1 billion in 1980, or 0.17 percent of the total receipts. By 1990, they may account for 0.20 percent of all business receipts. . . . Black firms will likely continue losing ground to white firms. In 1969, receipts of black firms were equal to 13.5 percent of total black income. By 1980, the share was down to 8.9 percent, and it may drop to 7 percent by 1990."[10]

The "black capitalism" model was, for a while, held up as a solution to the problem in many black communities. For example, the federal government initiated a number of business development programs in the 1960s, and many of these programs operated on the assumption that black communities could be stabilized by creating a black middle class who would support black business entrepreneurs. The fact that blacks owned few businesses in their neighborhoods was linked to the ghetto riots of the 1960s. Small, low-interest loans were made available starting in 1966 through the Small Business Administration (SBA) and the Office of Economic Opportunity (OEO). President Nixon in 1969 centralized all of the federal programs assisting minorities, created the Office of Minority Business Enterprise (OMBE), and his Executive Order 11458 created the Minority Business Development Agency (MBDA). Funding priorities included the establishment of Minority Enterprise Business Investment Companies (MESBIC), which provided venture capital and long-term financing for minority businesses. Community Development Corporations (CDC) were also established, under OEO's

Special Impact Program, to aid inner-city economic development. The Community Development Block Grant (CDBG) program was created in 1974 to replace the Model Cities and Urban Renewal programs.

Marshall and Swinton assessed the impact of federal economic development programs on the black community:

> The black capitalism programs have not been notably successful. As of 1975, 78 percent of all businesses in low-income black areas of central cities were owned by outsiders. Moreover, the programs and the agencies have been tainted by scandal and accusations of inefficiency. The default rates on the small business loans have been very high, and administrative regulations almost guarantee failure by restricting the size of the loans and limiting them to businesses which could not receive private financing.[11]

Earl Graves, the publisher and editor of *Black Enterprise,* has been a strong advocate for improving business development activities in the black community. He writes:

> Many federal programs were formed because of the failure of the private sector to address all the needs of the minority entrepreneurial community. Because of heightened social consciousness, many large corporations have made efforts on their own, or through the national Minority Supplier Development Council, to help bring small minority businesses into the mainstream.
>
> Removing the network of support that has been built over the years could have a disastrous impact on the black business community.
>
> Recent studies have shown that small businesses generated most of the new jobs in the country. Our only hope of developing the kind of political clout Black-Americans should have is through a strong black business sector that will provide the managerial and economic support for our diverse aspirations.
>
> In an atmosphere of ideological self-interest and budget cutting, the survival of the black business community depends on the support of ordinary citizens. Black business must recapture the loyalties of customers who were drawn away by changing work habits and lifestyles. Black business people must set highest standards of quality and service to meet the needs of black consumers.[12]

Black business owners play an essential role in the economic stability of the black community. Blacks buying black products provide needed revenue for these businesses to funnel back into black communities. Economist Robert S. Browne described the importance of black institutions in urban revitalization:

> The black financial institutions, because they are collectors of public savings, have clearly contributed more than any other black institution to the building of a black economic base, but because these financial institutions are heavily regulated and restricted by law, their contribution has been con-

servative in nature. They have enabled the black community to expand its home ownership base but have been less effective in encouraging a broader participation by blacks in the production, as opposed to the consumption side of the economy. But it is the production sector that the black community must establish if it is ever to achieve any extensive community revitalization.[13]

The 1980 Census revealed that the black population in the United States grew at a faster rate than did the total population. The 27.5 million blacks in the United States in 1980 represented a 17 percent increase over 1970, whereas the overall U.S. population grew by only 11.3 percent during the seventies.[14] The total income of the black population increased from $38.1 billion in 1969 to more than $144 billion in 1981, and $193.5 billion in 1985.[15]

Civil rights organizations such as the Reverend Jesse Jackson's PUSH (People United to Serve Humanity) and the NAACP (National Association for the Advancement of Colored People) have begun to awaken black consumers to the size and potential impact of their economic clout. These mainstream civil rights organizations have spearheaded "Buy Black" campaigns in an effort to help black-owned businesses. They have also threatened to use boycotts, picketing, and demonstrations, all of which fall under their "selective patronage" strategy, against those large corporations that have sizable black clientele (e.g., the fast food, soft drink, and liquor industries) but fail to invest in the black community.

The black leadership in America is searching for ways to attract new investment and new job-producing industries to central cities. They are searching for strategies (e.g., tax incentives, free trade zones, and other business inducements) to slow the economic disinvestment trend in many minority and low-income areas. Moreover, these organizations are attempting to inform the black community about how and where it spends its consumer dollars. Cleveland A. Chandler, a professor of economics at Howard University in Washington, D.C., described the issues that affect the economics of the black community:

> Blacks produced $175 billion worth of goods and services in 1981, which was 6.7 percent of the U.S. gross national product. Black labor, enterprise and nonhuman resources earned $141.4 billion in 1981. Black households received $144 billion in personal income in 1981, paid a total of $22.5 billion income taxes, spent $144.6 billion in markets for consumer goods and services, and saved about $6.8 billion.
>
> The black economy of the U.S. is indeed an economic resource that can work more to the benefit of black minority communities. . . . At this juncture, improvements in the shape of the black U.S. economy appear to be

more important than merely changing its size. The management and use of economic resources are more crucial for black survival, success, and security through the volume of income and wealth that flow into and out of our banks.[16]

Most of the nation's black-owned business firms are small operations. However, the number of black enterprises that have paid employees has grown over the years. Between 1972 and 1977, for example, the number of black-owned firms with paid employees increased by 63 percent (from 24,504 to 39,968).[17] This is not a small point when one considers the fact that the number of persons a company employs is related to the firm's stability. Lower failure rates among larger businesses have been found to be related more to the size of these firms than to economic cycles.[18]

Recessions in the general economy often leave depressionlike conditions in inner-city neighborhoods. Black and other small inner-city businesses are vulnerable when the economy is booming and are even more so in a sluggish economy. The stability of these small business firms is threatened by the high unemployment, poverty, and high crime rates that persist in inner-city minority neighborhoods.

LOCATION OF BLACK BUSINESS ENTERPRISES

The nation's black-owned business enterprises are concentrated in large metropolitan areas, and they experienced an impressive expansion from 1972 to 1982, despite economic recession and high inflation. The SMSAs that contained the largest number of black-owned business firms all experienced a net increase in the number of these firms between 1972 and 1977 and between 1977 and 1982. The ranking of black business firms (by the number of businesses) in the SMSAs shifted somewhat between 1972 and 1982. For example, the number of black businesses in the Houston SMSA was ranked seventh in 1972 and fifth in 1982.[19]

A 1982 survey of minority-owned businesses showed that only 10 percent of the black-owned businesses in the nation's major cities had paid employees in 1982. The average receipts of these firms varied from city to city. The highest average business receipts were recorded in Chicago ($74,247) and Atlanta ($68,293); the lowest average receipts per firm were recorded in Dallas ($27,515) and Houston ($28,318). Houston had more than three times as many black businesses as Atlanta in 1982. However, the gross receipts from Atlanta's 3,493 black-owned

Table 8.1. Distribution of Black-owned Houston Businesses, 1977 and 1982.

Classification	1977 Number	1977 Percent	1982 Number	1982 Percent
Agricultural	—	—	90	0.9
Construction	498	9.8	679	6.8
Manufacturing	39	0.8	52	0.5
Transportation and utilities	757	14.8	1,052	10.5
Wholesale trade	24	0.5	53	0.5
Retail trade	1,203	23.5	2,162	21.6
Finance, insurance, and real estate	214	4.2	409	4.1
Selected services	2,047	40.1	4,235	42.3
Other industries and not classified	322	6.3	1,287	12.8
Total	5,104	100.0	10,019	100.0

Source: U.S. Bureau of the Census, *1982 Survey of Minority-Owned Business Enterprises: Blacks* (Washington, D.C.: Government Printing Office, 1982).

firms were just 16 percent less than Houston's 10,019 black business firms. Houston ranked fourth among the major cities in terms of (1) the number of black-owned firms, (2) the number of black-owned firms with paid employees, and (3) the gross receipts generated by black-owned business enterprises (more than $283 million in 1982).[20] This figure represents a 100-percent increase in gross receipts generated by Houston's black businesses in a five-year period (i.e., from $141 million in 1977). The city's black firms continue to be clustered in the service and retail trade industries, which accounted for nearly two-thirds of Houston's black businesses in 1977 as well as 1982 (see Table 8.1). The distribution of black-owned businesses in Houston mirrors the national trend of underrepresentation in selected business classifications (manufacturing, wholesale, finance, insurance, and real estate).

As black communities across the nation attempt to stimulate reinvestment and redevelopment activities in declining areas, black lending institutions take on added importance in this process. Black-owned banks, savings and loan associations, and mortgage companies provide needed loans to black homeowners and business entrepreneurs in high-risk areas or in redlined neighborhoods, where lending institutions refuse to finance any projects. There were forty-eight black banks in the nation in 1980. Three of these were located in Texas: Riverside Bank in Houston, First Texas Bank in Dallas, and National Security Bank in Tyler. The economic recessions of the early and mid-eighties, however, had a devastating effect on two of them. National Security Bank was declared insolvent in 1982, and Riverside Bank closed its doors in 1985. In 1986, Houston celebrated its 150th birthday, the much-publicized sesquicentennial, without a single black-owned bank.

Houston's Riverside Bank was founded in 1963 and was located in the heart of the Third Ward. It was the nation's twenty-eighth largest black-owned bank in 1980, with assets of more than $15 million.[21] The bank increased its assets to more than $18.3 million in 1982, making it the twenty-fifth largest black-owned bank in the country at the time.[22] Although Houston emerged as the home of the largest urban black community in the South, Riverside Bank was one of the South's smallest black banks. A list of southern cities that had black banks in 1983 includes: (1) Atlanta's Citizens Trust Bank, assets of $61.9 million; (2) Durham's Mechanic and Farmers Bank, assets of $44.5 million; (3) Dallas's First Texas Bank, assets of $40.6 million; (4) New Orleans's Liberty Bank and Trust, assets of $40.6 million; (5) Richmond's Consolidated Bank and Trust, assets of $37.9 million; (6) Memphis's Tri-State Bank, assets of $34.1 million; (7) Nashville's Citizens Savings Bank, assets of $21.7 million; (8) Savannah's Carver State Bank, assets of $21.7 million; and (9) Jacksonville's Century National Bank, assets of $19.4 million.[23]

Hard economic times combined with low black patronage figured largely in the demise of Riverside Bank. Low black patronage can be attributed largely to the social changes that occurred in the sixties. When Riverside Bank was founded in the early sixties, civil rights issues were on the national agenda, but Houston lagged behind cities that were in the forefront of the civil rights movement. Houston's black leadership was conservative compared with the leaders in such cities as Birmingham, Montgomery, Atlanta, Memphis, Nashville, and Richmond; this was apparent in the fact that Houston was one of the only major cities in the nation that did not explode in the sixties, even after the assassination of Dr. Martin Luther King, Jr., in 1968. Strong loyalties between Houston's large and conservative black community and its black bank never materialized. The opposite was true in Richmond, which had a black bank as early as 1903, Nashville in 1904, and Atlanta in 1921. Public accommodation concessions were made by city government and local businesses to black Houstonians in the sixties. These concessions further weakened the economic bond between Riverside Bank and the black community. The black community expanded and became more decentralized, moving outside the traditional wards, in the

Businessman Mack H. Hannah (photograph by Earlie Hudnall).

seventies and eighties. This population expansion was in part due to the in-migration of individuals from outside the region who had little knowledge of or few loyalties to Riverside Bank.

There were only thirty-seven black savings and loan associations in the United States in 1982, with one, Standard Savings and Loan Association, operating in Texas. Standard Savings was founded in 1958 by Mack H. Hannah, one of Houston's pioneering black business entrepreneurs.[24] It was the fourteenth largest black savings and loan business in 1982, with assets of more than $17.9 million and $18.9 million in 1983.[25] Located on Dowling Street in the heart of Houston's Third Ward, Standard Savings also operates branch offices in two other primarily black Houston neighborhoods.

It is worth noting that 1983 was the first time that more than one black-owned Houston firm had a spot on the coveted Top 100 list compiled by *Black Enterprise* magazine. The two Houston firms were Smith Pipe Companies, Inc. (ranked fourteenth) and Frenchy's Po-Boy (ranked eighty-ninth). Smith Pipe in 1980 was the seventh largest black-owned company in the United States. Founded by George Smith, this company experienced phenomenal growth in a relatively short period of time, booming along with Houston's oil-supported economy. In 1980, the company employed 133 persons and had its highest gross sales: more than $48 million. The economic woes of the oil industry, beginning in 1981, had a dramatic impact on small oil supply firms such as Smith Pipe. The company's sales dropped to $35 million in 1982 and to less than $4 million in 1983. The firm did not appear on the 1984 *Black Enterprise* Top 100 list. More than four hundred black- and Hispanic-owned oil supply firms in southeast Texas went out of business in the oil-glut recession. Smith Pipe was one of the few minority oil supply firms in Texas that were able to survive the recession.[26]

Frenchy's Po-Boy, Houston's other firm that has made the *Black Enterprise* Top 100 (it first made the list in 1983), replaced Smith Pipe as the largest black-owned business in Houston. This family-owned restaurant, specializing in Louisiana Creole-style foods, was founded in 1969 by Percy (Frenchy) and Sallie Creuzot and now employs more than three hundred persons. Frenchy's had gross sales of $8.3 million in 1982 and $9.5 million in 1984. The original Frenchy's restaurant is located on Scott Street (between Texas Southern University and the University of Houston) in Houston's Third Ward. The business has been expanding since 1979 at the rate of two new restaurants per year. By the summer of 1984, Frenchy's had expanded to eleven locations in the Houston area.[27]

Frenchy's is probably the best local example of a small black-owned fast food business moving beyond the traditional boundaries of Houston's black community. Frenchy's Creole fried chicken has been successful in breaking the racial barrier, a major hurdle facing most black business entrepreneurs.

The center of Houston's black business activity has shifted over the past four decades, along with the city's changing black population. The hub of the city's black business and economic life was first located in the Freedmen's Town/Fourth Ward area through the 1940s; the bulk of black business activity shifted in the 1950s to the Fifth Ward, which grew significantly after World War II. During the sixties and early seventies the black business center shifted again, to the Third Ward. The Third Ward in the mid-eighties had a wide range of black business enterprises, including most of the city's black financial, real estate, and professional services. The neighborhood's proximity to Houston's central business district and to the Medical Center made it an ideal location for commercial and residential development. Carolyn Jenkins's study of business and economic development activities in the Third Ward disclosed that business owners of all races expressed a high degree of confidence in the area; they viewed revitalization and the in-migration of affluent persons into the neighborhood as "good for business." [28]

Jenkins also described the issue of absentee business ownership in the Third Ward. She writes:

> Ownership of businesses in the inner-city neighborhoods continues to be a subject of concern in most areas. In Houston's Third Ward, a predominantly black neighborhood, a majority of the business owners live outside the neighborhood. However, when residency is analyzed by race of business owner, black business owners were more likely to reside in the neighborhood (54.3 percent) as compared to their white counterparts (17.9 percent). . . . Small business owners who live in the area seem to have a close affinity for the neighborhood not only for conducting business, but also as a place to live and raise their families.
>
> Business owners who live in the Third Ward were more likely to hire persons from the Third Ward as compared with those owners who live outside the neighborhood. [29]

The findings of a 1983 survey of black-owned Houston firms provide an in-depth analysis of local black entrepreneurship. [30] A demographic profile of two hundred randomly selected black-owned Houston firms revealed that less than one-half (43.5 percent) of the owners were native Houstonians; a majority (54.5 percent) of black firms were "new arrivals" to business (i.e., their operations were less than ten years old); six

Above: The original Frenchy's Po-Boy Restaurant on Scott Street in the Third Ward, 1983 (photograph by Earlie Hudnall). *Below:* Houston Citizens Chamber of Commerce, 1984 (photograph by Earlie Hudnall).

of every ten firms surveyed had expanded over the previous three years; more than 82 percent of the firms employed ten or fewer employees; and nearly nine of every ten firms studied continued to be dependent upon black consumers for their economic livelihood.

Houston's black business enterprises play a marginal role relative to the city's entire economy. However, these business operations play significant roles in stabilizing many declining black inner-city neighborhoods. While business opportunities have been expanding for black and other minorities, the barriers that limit minority business formation remain, and black business leaders still see the need for having their own business associations. Houston's Citizens Chamber of Commerce was founded in the thirties, when Jim Crow restrictions were law. This black business organization's endurance for more than fifty years is testimony to the area's dual opportunity structure. There is a growing consensus among business, political, and community leaders that economic and civil rights issues in the eighties are synonymous. Black business and professional organizations are faced with the monumental task of formulating and implementing strategies to redirect black consumer dollars and other economic resources to central cities communities where blacks are concentrated. This economic challenge may well emerge as the major issue facing blacks in the next several decades.

A PLAN OF ACTION

Small, independently owned business firms will likely play a greater role in bolstering the nation's economy and the vitality of the inner cities as we move toward the twenty-first century. The United States does not have an economic development master plan or an urban policy that could reverse this country's declining central cities. In the absence of such a plan or policy, the black community in Houston and other cities will need to create development strategies that will enable their constituents to become economically self-sufficient. Small business enterprises should be a major element of this strategy. Some goals for economic improvement are included in the following eleven-point "Black Development Plan":

1. Inasmuch as black business and the black community are tied together, it appears that a necessary ingredient for the continued survival

of both rests with rechanneling the monies that tend to flow out of black areas and to maximize those resources which blacks control.

2. Neighborhood revitalization in black areas will need to be developed in a number of sectors, namely: (a) residential development, (b) commercial ventures, (c) job training and employment for residents, (d) emphasis on land, home, and business ownerships, and (e) municipal services and capital improvements to be coordinated with the redevelopment plan.

3. To achieve neighborhood redevelopment, the black business community will need to diversify itself in the production sector of the economy as opposed to the consumption sector. Black business diversification may take the form of expanded services and products as well as joint ventures and franchises.

4. Black financial institutions will need to continue supporting the establishment of black firms, particularly in redlined areas. In addition, tougher regulations and stiffer penalties are needed for those institutions which engage in redlining. Without lender confidence in an area, that area will likely remain economically unstable and experience decline.

5. Black business associations will need to become more aggressive in their recruitment of members as well as in selling their programs to prospective members, residents in the neighborhood, and to the larger non-minority community. Increased public awareness is needed to educate the community on the role and function of black business organizations.

6. The black business community, in conjunction with neighborhood residents and other civic organizations, needs to develop mechanisms to reduce crime, fear of crime, and drug trafficking in the community. These groups have a vested interest in ensuring that their neighborhoods are safe.

7. A close monitoring of black business failures needs to be undertaken; reasons for business failures and possible impact on the neighborhood might also be addressed in this process.

8. Residential and business displacement, and business takeovers within the black community should be investigated. The central thrust of such a strategy would be to determine the extent to which displacement is occurring and ascertain a demographic profile of new owners.

9. A number of civil rights organizations including the People United to Serve Humanity (PUSH) have been successful in signing economic development agreements, also known as "covenants," with major corporations. PUSH, led by the Reverend Jesse Jackson, publicized their "selective patronage" strategy by the threat of boycotts, picketing, and

demonstrations against companies who failed to cooperate. Reverend Jackson was also armed with up-to-date market research on the volume of money spent by blacks on a given product. This proved to be a potent weapon in persuading large corporations to assist in economic development activities in the black community. The food, soft drink, and liquor industries were the initial targets, and agreements were expanded to include other companies doing business with and in the black community. The first agreement was reached with General Foods in 1972. PUSH subsequently negotiated agreements with Joseph Schlitz Brewing Company, the Seven-Up Company, the Burger King Corporation, Heublein, Inc., and the Coca-Cola Company.[31] The strategy that PUSH employed is becoming a real economic weapon as black purchasing power increases. Black consumers have the potential for redirecting billions of dollars back into economic development projects which are needed in most black communities.

10. Black businesses will need to seek new markets as the black population becomes more decentralized and suburban.

11. Finally, close monitoring of public monies (i.e., federal block grants and other "poverty" funds) that have been targeted for low-income areas is needed to ensure that these shrinking dollars are not diverted into the more affluent "downtown" projects and away from the areas of greatest need.

This eleven-point development plan is not meant to be all-inclusive. However, it does provide a general framework from which individuals and groups can begin to analyze development strategies for the black community. Because many of the problems that exist in Houston are common to other cities, strategies for black economic development have wide implications for black communities across the nation.

9.

Law Enforcement
and the Black Community

Houston's crime problem is not unlike that found in other major American cities, although Houston's was exacerbated during the 1970–80 period by the city's rapid growth in population and land area, the tendency of many neighborhood residents to move frequently, and the city's limited police force.[1]

This chapter examines a number of key issues that relate to police roles and law-enforcement strategies, crime and inner-city neighborhoods, and police-citizen relations in the black community.

POLICE ROLES AND THE INNER CITY

Society creates contrasting roles for the police, that is, many aspects of police functions are mutually contradictory and thus place the police officer attempting to carry out his or her roles in a serious dilemma. Police responsibilities are broad, encompassing more than just a concern with criminal behavior. The police are expected to assume direct responsibility for maintaining law and order and, at the same time, to protect the lives and property of citizens. Performance of police work is sometimes viewed as synonymous with force. Police operate under the basic philosophy that it is their obligation to "enforce" the law and to use the necessary "force" to deal with given situations.[2] David Jacobs described the coercive maintenance function of the police: "In this society, the major institution responsible for the coercive maintenance of stability is the police. . . . In general, it can be said that the modern police force is a reactive agency with limited capacity to detect or prevent the many illegal activities which are comparatively inconspicuous."[3]

Quite often, the maintenance-of-order function of the police defines their role in terms of exercising discretion in life-and-death situations. Maintenance of order also requires a partnership between police and community residents; neglect by either group can fragment this delicate balance into warring or isolated enclaves that are unable or unwilling to communicate with each other. A major source of strain in inner-city neighborhoods results from challenges to the "establishment," which continually place the police (who are the maintainers of the establishment) and inner-city and minority residents in confrontation. Historically, the urban poor have disliked and distrusted the police, and the feeling has been reciprocated. Inner-city residents and the police often find themselves misunderstood, mistreated, and maligned.[4]

A primary reason for this antipathy is that ghetto residents often perceive the police as outsiders and protectors of the propertied class. Lee P. Brown addressed this issue of the police officers' function and the black community:

> The structure (and mission) of the police in America does not have roots in the protection of the rights of black people. Nor have black people had a voice in determining the police role. Furthermore, the police have not attempted to become a part of the black community and sincerely win its support. Rather, the police have developed as their role the protection of life and property. In respect to the first mission, the protection of life, this turns out in reality to be the protection of white lives from blacks. . . . The role of protecting property also serves to exclude the black community from being a part of the police's favorable concern. When the police patrol the white community, they are in fact protecting the property of that community. . . . The property which the police do "protect" in the black community is likely to belong to a white absentee landowner. Thus, the service he renders in that regard is not a service for the black community, but a service for a business-man that leaves the community each night. Hence, within the black community, the police are indeed looked upon as an occupying army protecting the interests of the ruling class in a neo-colonial setting.[5]

There can be little doubt that the poor are also benefactors of expanded police service. However, it is unlikely that the poor benefit as much as wealthier citizens. Specifically, affluent persons contribute a proportionally smaller amount of their income for police services than do those at the lower end of the economic spectrum, whose housing costs (and property taxes) take up a larger share of their income and when the sales tax, which is regressive, is taken into account. Thus, a strong police force not only helps to preserve the social and economic advantages of the affluent, but also costs them less.[6] In poor, inner-city

Table 9.1. Residents' and Police Officers' Perceptions of Police Roles.

Role	Percent Suggesting Ideal Role		Percent Suggesting Real Role	
	Police	Resident	Police	Resident
Protection of life and property	43	45	33	13
Prevention of crime	14	18	11	18
Enforcement of laws	25	20	30	16
Public service	13	8	14	8
Apprehension of criminals	4	5	12	47
Don't know	1	4	0	3
Percentage totals	100	100	100	100
Total (N)	(100)	(100)	(100)	(100)

Source: K. L. Sindwani and R. D. Bullard, *Police Roles in the Inner-City* (Houston: Texas Southern University Report Series, 1977).

areas, traditional policing strategies are considered by black residents to be "overpolicing" and "underprotecting."[7] These terms have meant police arrival in force, show of force, and use of force. The National Advisory Commission on Civil Disorders (the Kerner Commission) cited excessive use of force—police brutality—as a major contributing factor to the urban civil disturbances of the 1960s. Since then, blacks have challenged the police's excessive use of force through litigation and political mobilization, which resulted in the election of black mayors who in turn appointed black police chiefs.

While police are involved in protection of life and property functions, crime prevention, and enforcement of laws, they are also involved in noncriminal, emergency, and social service functions. The role of the police officer as a public servant who often must intervene and resolve interpersonal conflicts has been underemphasized. The diverse expectations and often contradictory roles are at the heart of many conflicts surrounding police-community relations in inner-city neighborhoods.

An illustration of the differences of opinion separating Houston inner-city residents and the police can be found in a 1977 study that analyzed each side's evaluation of the "ideal" and "real" police roles.[8] The data in this study were drawn from one hundred white police officers randomly selected from the Houston Police Department and one hundred black residents of an inner-city neighborhood. The data in Table 9.1 indicate that the police and black inner-city residents expressed similar views on the ideal roles that officers should play in their neighborhood, specifically, the protection, enforcement, and prevention functions. The apprehension and public service functions were rated as lesser ideal roles by both groups.

The police and inner-city residents showed a marked difference in their evaluations of the "real" role (or actual performance) of the police. The protection and enforcement functions were the major roles police saw themselves actually performing. On the other hand, residents tended to view the everyday performance of police to be basically the apprehension of alleged criminals. It appears that there is a wide discrepancy between the roles black inner-city residents would like police to perform and their actual performance. Inner-city residents expect police to assume the role of "protector," but tend to view the police as acting "after the fact," that is, apprehending lawbreakers.

HOUSTON'S BOOMING CRIME AND FEAR OF CRIME

Crime and fear of victimization can alter the life-styles of nearly all Americans. The element of fear has reached a point where many homes have become "armed camps" and where the "end result is disfigurement of society and downgrading of the quality of life."[9] Crime in a city the size of Houston means that thousands of people are affected, and during the boom years of the 1970s, the number of major crimes jumped 84 percent.[10] The largest increases were in rape and motor vehicle theft, although the homicide rate showed a dramatic increase as well (see Table 9.2).

Table 9.3 shows another factor responsible for the atmosphere of fear

Table 9.2. Reported Offenses in Houston, 1970 and 1980.[a]

	1970	1980	Actual Change	Percent Change
Homicide	356	651	+ 295	+ 82.8
Rape	411	1,446	+ 1,035	+252.0
Robbery	6,405	10,875	+ 4,470	+ 69.8
Aggravated assault	2,746	2,853	+ 107	+ 3.8
Burglary	25,626	49,315	+23,689	+ 92.4
Theft	29,007	50,780	+21,773	+ 75.1
Vehicle theft	13,573	28,166	+14,593	+107.5
Totals	78,124	144,086	+65,962	+ 87.4

Source: Houston Police Department, *Assessment of the Department Problems and Issues* (Houston: Houston Police Department, 1982), table IV.
[a] All crime figures are based on Actual Part I Index Offenses as reported in Uniform Crime Report.

Table 9.3. Ranking of Police Officers per 1,000 Population, by City.

City	Population	Sworn Personnel	No. Officers Incorporated per square mile	Area (square miles)	No. Officers per 1,000
Washington	635,000	3,720	55	68	5.8
Philadelphia	1,600,000	7,400	57	129	4.6
Chicago	3,005,072	12,684	55	230	4.2
Baltimore	870,000	3,172	37	86	3.6
Detroit	1,203,339	4,129	29	140	3.4
New York	7,071,639	23,505	73	320	3.3
Los Angeles	2,996,358	6,865	15	470	2.3
Dallas	910,000	1,974	5	378	2.2
Phoenix	807,316	1,647	5	331	2.0
Houston	1,600,000	3,192	6	556	1.9

Source: Houston Police Department, *Assessment of the Department Problems and Issues* (Houston: Houston Police Department, 1982), table X.

and the surge in crime statistics: the low visibility of the police. The problem is not simply Houston's traditionally low citizen/police ratio. The greater problem was the city's policy of voracious annexation. The extension of Houston's city limits strained city services delivery (e.g., fire and police protection, garbage collection) and was achieved at the expense of many heavily minority inner-city neighborhoods.[11] In the 556 square miles of the city, the sight of an HPD patrol car could be a rare one indeed.[12] Philadelphia, with a 1980 population about equal in size to that of Houston, had twice as many officers and an area to cover that was only about one-fourth the size of Houston.

The Houston police force is sparse throughout the city, but crime and neighborhood security (or lack of security) are of special concern in Houston's inner city, where business owners and residents live in fear because of their increasing vulnerability; nationally, more than one-fourth of all ghetto businesses are burglarized each year.[13] James E. Blackwell, in his book *The Black Community: Diversity and Unity,* assessed the problem of crime in inner-city neighborhoods: "Robberies, burglaries, shoplifting, and other felonious activities place a heavy financial toll on businesses in ghettos and central cities of America. Hence, such crimes have serious consequences for the overall economy of the black community (businesses are forced to relocate and to pay higher insurance rates and higher prices for poorer services)."[14]

A number of attempts have been made to solve the crime and fear of crime problem in the nation's cities. For example, the Law Enforcement Assistance Administration (LEAA) was created when Congress enacted the Omnibus Crime Control and Safe Streets Act of 1968, intended to control urban unrest and rising crime rates. It was designed to strengthen the operation of local and state law enforcement agencies, supply state and local governments with block grants to improve their criminal justice systems, sponsor and evaluate research, and provide funding for the training and education of criminal justice personnel.

Many local and state agencies used their initial grants to purchase hardware and equipment. A number of wide-ranging, well-financed nationwide anti-crime programs were funded by the LEAA. Grants were also made to local community organizations for demonstration programs, usually one year in duration. Houston's Third Ward Victim-Witness Program was initiated in April of 1981 with a $30,000 grant from LEAA. This federally funded neighborhood program was designed to "overcome attitudes born of distrust of police, fear of retribution from criminals released by an overloaded justice system, and a sense that crime is a constant, inevitable part of life." [15] This grass-roots crime program was a one-year demonstration project and in its short duration had a negligible effect on the neighborhood's overall security. The funding of the Third Ward Victim-Witness Program, however, typified the shortsighted nature of the LEAA and the futility of short-term assistance in dealing with the complex problem of crime. The LEAA did not meet its principal goal of crime reduction because the root causes of crime extend well beyond the criminal justice system. Urban migration, persistent unemployment, a sluggish economy, crowded housing conditions, poverty, family disorganization, mistrust of police, and a host of other factors are all implicated in the urban crime problem.[16]

Another attempt was made in 1983 to address the "poorly designed policing strategies" in the Third Ward.[17] The Houston Police Department designed and implemented in March, 1983, a pilot decentralized patrol program known as DART (Directed Area Responsibility Team), another one-year experimental program. The goals of this neighborhood-oriented crime reduction program included the following:

> To establish a closer, more positive relationship between Houston's police officers and the communities and neighborhoods they serve.
> To reduce citizens' fear of crime by crime prevention techniques, security surveys, and victim assistance programs.
> To increase community involvement in police activities through special programs, meetings, and permanently assigned officers to specific neighborhood areas.
> To increase job satisfaction, enhance job recruitment, and improve mo-

rale by allowing officers to participate in the decision-making process regarding strategies and tactics.[18]

Preliminary results from the program's first operational month revealed the following: (1) response time of DART patrol units (which averaged about 4.9 minutes from dispatch to arrival at the scene) was faster than in any other section of the city, and (2) the DART program's evening shift cleared nearly 19 percent of the crimes reported to that shift; this figure compared favorably with the department's overall crime clearance rate of 16 percent in 1981.[19] The pilot DART program was judged a success, and in 1986 covered Houston's Third Ward, the Medical Center area, and the Rice University area.

CONFRONTATION BETWEEN BLACK AND BLUE

Discriminatory practices and racism have not been eliminated from the administration of justice. Such practices tend to perpetuate the ill feelings between black citizens and the police. Likewise, the police often look upon the black community with a less than favorable attitude. Blackwell asserts: "Evidence suggests that approximately 75 percent of white police officers assigned to predominantly black precincts expressed some form of prejudice or antipathy toward black people. About 10 percent of black officers assigned to predominantly black precincts harbor extreme anti-black attitudes. . . . Once confronted by the police, blacks frequently claim to be subjected to status degradation, physical and verbal abuse, and to be referred to in terms of racial epithets." [20]

Several major factors contribute to the problem of police-community (black) relations: (1) the recruitment of officers from the "undereducated and politically conservative ranks" of white society and (2) the underrepresentation of blacks on the police force.[21] The institutional nature of police conduct toward the black community should not be underestimated, and allegations of police abuse and misconduct cannot be dismissed as mere instances of an overactive imagination on the part of black citizens. Lee P. Brown, Houston's first black police chief, wrote about the problem of police brutality before he came to Houston to head the city's police force. He stated: "Within the black community, police harassment, police brutality, and police corruption do exist. The abuses do not accidentally occur and they are not acts of malice on the part of the individual. The abuses are built into the police system by virtue of its composition and organization structure, and maintained by the articulation of the police mission. Void of power, the black community remains the unfortunate recipient of misuse by police authority." [22]

The Houston Police Department has remained largely a white force over the years. The first black officer on the Houston police force was hired in the late 1940s, at the insistence of the Harris County Council of Organizations (HCCO), a black political and civil rights organization. By 1960, there were 39 black officers on the 1,000-member force; black officers numbered 53 (out of a total of 1,654) in 1970; [23] 1980 data showed 215 black officers out of a 3,200-person police force. As of September, 1983, there were 272 blacks on the city's police force (about 8.5 percent of the total). [24]

The issue of blacks on the Houston police force is rarely discussed from an economic perspective. For example, employment as a Houston police officer allowed an inexperienced high-school graduate to obtain a starting salary in 1983 of $20,000. Thus, underrepresentation of blacks on the police force means a significant loss of black purchasing power. For example, a total of 896 black officers out of 3,200 would be needed to reach "parity," that is, a percentage that reflects the number of blacks in the city's total population. With 28 percent of the city's residents being black, the Houston Police Department in 1983 was below parity by 624 black officers. Moreover, for every 100 black officers *not* hired by the city, a minimum of $2 million is lost in potential black purchasing power. In economic terms, an additional 624 black rookie police officers on Houston's police force would boost the city's annual black buying power by nearly $12.5 million. Thus, there is strong economic argument for having more black police officers (particularly as jobs become more scarce), as well as the traditional social and cultural arguments for having a police force that is representative of the community.

Houston installed its first black police chief, Dr. Lee P. Brown, with the election of Kathy Whitmire as mayor of Houston in 1980. The appointment of Chief Brown by the mayor was perceived as a political victory by the black community, but Brown received a less than enthusiastic endorsement from the city's mostly white police force. However, the city's Afro-American Patrolmen's League did give the new chief its support. Black police officers for a number of years had registered complaints of discrimination and differential treatment in hiring and promotion. Prior to Chief Brown's appointment, no black Houston police offi-

Houston Police Chief Lee P. Brown, 1983 (photograph courtesy of the Texas Southern University Archives).

cer had risen above the rank of sergeant; the department in 1983 had one black lieutenant.

Police conduct in Houston's black community has been a sore point for years. The confrontations between police and black citizens frequently raise the question of how many blacks were beaten.[25] Tom Abernathy, a white reporter for the *Houston Press,* commented on life in Houston's "Little Harlem," the Fourth Ward, in the thirties. His observations, though somewhat stereotypical (if not racist), do illustrate the peculiar nature of the black community–white police relations.

> The street [West Dallas] assumes an air of sudden tension as a white policeman saunters along his beat. The loafers hush their loud talking and the crowd in the barber shops and cafes sink into the shell Negroes assume as a protection against the ways of the white man's laws.
>
> The officer stops at one large group. "Better move on boys," he says in a kindly tone.
>
> The group breaks up and the policeman saunters on into the next block. Within five minutes, they are back together again, their tongues wagging as before. They do not comment on the officer, but seem glad to get back into the sunshine.[26]

The Houston police have a long history of abuse against the city's black citizens. For example, the infamous Houston Race Riot of 1917 was touched off following "a period of rising racial tension" heightened by an altercation between white police officers and black military police from Camp Logan, a black military encampment.[27] Edgar Schuler related the sequence of events of the Houston riot:

> It began with the arrest of a Negro woman, drunk and therefore using abusive language, by the white policemen Sparks and Daniels. In this process they treated her with considerable severity, if not actual brutality, as a result of which Edwards, a Negro soldier (a private, but also a provost guard) attempted to intervene. This led to his beating, arrest, and incarceration, but as he was not kept long at the station, he was able to be back at the camp in the late morning.
>
> Early in the afternoon, Corporal Baltimore, another provost guard, attempted to locate the police officers stationed in the San Felipe district (Fourth Ward) to find out what had happened to Edwards and why. Directed by another Negro soldier, he soon located officers Sparks and Daniels. Being refused the information he sought, he attempted to escape from the policemen, was chased, shot at, captured, beaten, arrested, taken to the station, and locked up in the early afternoon. . . . The story of Baltimore's ill treatment at the hands of the same policemen who had that morning beaten up Edwards had been carried back to the camp. . . . Broadcast throughout the camp by the grapevine, and at the same time exaggerated, this news proved to be the straw that broke the camel's back. For it tended to confirm the al-

ready current notion that the only way to release the cumulative pressure of resentment and rage was to retaliate directly against the offending San Felipe policemen.[28]

In an effort to "punish" the Houston police, weapons were seized from the Camp Logan armory, and a group of seventy-five to one hundred black soldiers went on a raid in Houston. The aftermath of the August 23, 1917, riot left a death toll of twenty-five policemen, two white soldiers, four black soldiers, one Hispanic, and eight white civilians.[29] A military court-martial was conducted which was "only a slight pretense of a trial."[30] Thirteen black soldiers were hanged for murder and an additional forty-one received life sentences. Two subsequent trials were held, with an additional twelve soldiers receiving life sentences and sixteen receiving death sentences. Black Americans were outraged and "many men of the Twenty-fourth Infantry swore vengeance on the officials whom they accused of unjust treatment."[31] President Woodrow Wilson later commuted ten of the sixteen death sentences to life in prison.[32]

While other major cities exploded during the turbulent 1960s, Houston did not experience a major riot. However, a conflict did erupt in the spring of 1967 between Houston police and Texas Southern University students. The violence at the predominantly black university stemmed from police actions, protest activities, previous disorders in the city, and the administration of justice. The Kerner Commission classified the disturbance at Texas Southern University as a "serious disorder."[33] The circumstances that contributed to the disorder were described by the Kerner Commission:

> On May 16, two separate Negro protests were taking place in Houston. One group was picketing a garbage dump (Holmes Road Dump) in a Negro residential neighborhood, where a Negro child had drowned. Another was demonstrating at a junior high school on the grounds that Negro students were disciplined more harshly than white.
>
> That evening, college students who had participated in the protests returned to the campus of Texas Southern University. About 50 of them were grouped around a 29-year-old student, D. W., a Viet Nam Veteran, who was seeking to stimulate further protest action. A dispute broke out, and D. W. reportedly slapped another student. When the student threatened D. W., he left, armed himself with a pistol, and returned.
>
> In response to the report of a disturbance, two unmarked police cars with four officers arrived. Two of the officers questioned D. W., discovered he was armed with a pistol, and arrested him.
>
> A short time later, when one of the police cars returned to the campus, it was met by rocks and bottles thrown by students. A police officer called for

reinforcements; sporadic gunshots reportedly came from the men's dormitory. The police returned fire.

For several hours, gunfire punctuated unsuccessful attempts by community leaders to negotiate a truce between the students and the police.

When several tar barrels were set afire in the street, and shouting broke out again, police decided to enter the dormitory. A patrolman, struck by a ricocheting bullet, was killed. After clearing 480 occupants from the building, police searched it and found one shotgun and two .22 caliber pistols. The origin of the shot that killed the officer was not determined.[34]

While the police were clearing the students from the men's dormitory, the law enforcement officers destroyed several thousand dollars worth of the students' personal property. This overt retaliation by the police intensified the already growing animosity between City Hall and the black community.[35]

Further polarization of the black community and the Houston police occurred in the early 1970s, after the beating deaths of two black auto-theft suspects by two white police officers. In addition, a confrontation developed between a militant black group—People's Party II—and the police in the Third Ward. This incident is commonly referred to as the "Dowling Street Shootout," in which the chairman of People's Party II, twenty-one-year-old Carl Hamilton, was fatally shot by the police. This killing sparked protest from a large segment of Houston's black community. Police Chief Herman Short's resignation was demanded. However, Mayor Louie Welch did not yield to the pressure and kept Short on as chief of police.[36] Lee P. Brown addressed the ineffectiveness of such citizen protest. He wrote: "Traditionally, when a group launches a protest against the police, they direct their efforts toward the Chief of Police. To their surprise, nothing happens. This is because the Chief of Police is subordinate to, and often serves as, a buffer for the Chief Administrative Officer of the city—City Manager or Mayor. It is the elected officials that are vulnerable to public criticism, and not necessarily the Chief of Police."[37]

Despite the improvement that may have been made in the relations between Houston's police and the black community, there remains a degree of fear and mistrust of law enforcement officers in the inner city. A 1981 survey of 165 black residents from an inner-city Houston neighborhood revealed that nearly one-half of the respondents felt that fear of police, abusive and insulting language by police, and use of excessive force by police were problems in the black community.[38] Moreover, lower-income black residents gave higher severity ratings for the police-related problems than did middle-income citizens (see Table 9.4). These

Table 9.4. Residents' Perceptions of Police Conduct toward Black
Citizens.

Actions and Police Conduct	Residents' Perceptions[a]		
	No Problem	Small Problem	Severe Problem
Use of excessive force	44.6%	37.4%	18.0%
Acting discourteously toward black citizens	49.6%	31.7%	18.7%
Use of ethnic slurs	54.0%	32.4%	13.7%
Use of insulting language	41.1%	29.1%	19.9%
Slow response to calls in black neighborhoods	29.1%	29.1%	41.8%

Source: R. D. Bullard, *Fear of Crime, Fear of Police and Black Residents' Endorsement of Crime-Reduction Strategies* (Houston: Texas Southern University Publication, 1981), table III.
[a] The percentages are based on a sample of 165 black Houston residents.

differences are probably due to the frequency and context of the interactions of black lower-income and middle-income persons with the police, and to the nature of the police calls that emanate from the two income groups.

While many black citizens may suspect that there is a police policy of systematically stopping "suspicious-looking" persons (who happen to be black), proving that such a policy exists is an almost impossible task. Such an occasion did arise, however, in the winter of 1982 when two white Houston Police Department homicide detectives, D. E. Calhoun and R. G. Parish, issued an "unofficial" directive to officers regarding members of the Rastafarian religious group. The following message was written on City of Houston stationery and posted on the police bulletin board:

> All officers be advised that there is a religious cult in the Houston area calling themselves "Rastafarians." This cult, which is made up entirely of blacks, began in Jamaica and has approximately 50,000 members in the U.S. and approximately 250–300 members in the Houston area. Very little is known about the Rastafarians in this geographic area, although they are recognized as organized crime figures in the New York vicinity, where they are known for their narcotics and gun running activities and their almost daily shoot-outs with police officers.
>
> Members of the Rastafarians can be identified by the way in which they wear their hair. They do not believe in cutting their hair and wear it in long curls called "dreadlocks." Street talk around New York and Miami has it that some members of this cult are being trained in Cuba as terrorists.
>
> The Rastafarian religion teaches that their members should steal and that the Catholic Church is their enemy and that the Pope should be assassinated.

The Rastafarians are known to carry weapons and should be considered dangerous.

Any officer having any information, such as names, D.O.B.'s [dates of birth], or known hang-outs of the Rastafarians, are asked to call Detectives Calhoun or Parish, homicide, evenings.

After a defense attorney's accidental discovery of this document that circulated within the Houston Police Department, it generated a barrage of criticism from the community. Community meetings were held to outline strategies for dealing with the inflammatory memorandum, as well as the allegations of harassment of blacks who frequented reggae clubs in the city. Community groups and individual citizens took their complaints to the Houston City Council, where they voiced opposition to the two police officers' declaration of "open season" on Rastafarians and blacks who wear their hair in dreadlocks. The mayor and city council directed the police department to correct the statements issued by the two officers. Chief Lee P. Brown, on December 9, 1982, issued a memorandum that recalled the unofficial directive and attempted to correct the inaccurate characterization of Rastafarians presented in the Calhoun and Parish memorandum.

It is difficult to assess the damage caused by the two white officers' targeting of blacks for special surveillance. Their actions heightened the fears of many blacks and reinforced the belief that there still existed a double standard of justice for blacks and whites.

10.

The Quest
for Equal Rights

The struggle for equal rights continues, contrary to the rhetoric of neo-conservatives (some of whom are black) who claim that racial discrimination is a thing of the past. There are numerous studies and documentation to refute the claim that class is now the sole hurdle in blacks' struggle for parity in the larger society.[1] Institutional discrimination has not been eliminated from our society despite the numerous court orders, legislative acts, and directives. Thus, blacks in Houston, as well as in other areas in the nation, have come to recognize the shifting emphasis on and government commitment to human rights. Moreover, black organizations and their leaders have also shifted or adjusted their emphases and strategies to formulate economic-oriented agendas. However, the goals of equity and fairness remain the cornerstone of the human rights movement within the larger black community.

This chapter explores a number of key elements of black Houstonians' quest for first-class citizenship in Houston and in American society. The major subareas explored include evolving black leadership types, civil rights, equal educational opportunity, and black political empowerment.

EVOLVING BLACK LEADERSHIP

The traditional black leadership structure in the United States emerged largely as a response to institutionalized racism, "Jim Crowism," and to white-black race relations (e.g., superordinate-subordinate relationships) that grew out of slavery. Leadership, on a general level, has been defined as "the self-conscious capacity to provide vision and values, and practice which satisfies human needs and aspirations and transforms persons and society in the process." Black leaders are those individuals who "are or have been actively engaged in the solution of some common problems or the achievement of specific social goals."[2] Historically, the black church emerged as the major institution in the training and production of black leaders. To see this, one has only to observe the background of the black leaders who have been in the forefront of the civil rights movement in this country.

Black religious leadership embodied the characteristics of sociologist Dennis Poplin's three leadership types: (1) institutional leaders, that is, persons who hold positions that are generally thought to have authority, (2) grass-roots leaders, community activists, human and civil rights advocates, and special interest representatives, and (3) power elite leaders, or individuals whose influence is derived from their economic independence.[3] The black church provided the black minister a degree of economic independence which surpassed that of other black professionals. Houston's Rev. Jack Yates typified this role of the black minister. He was the pastor of Antioch Baptist Church and one of the most influential local black leaders in the late 1800s. It was the black church leadership that initiated the laying of the cobblestone streets in the Fourth Ward in response to the city fathers' refusal to pave streets in black areas; it was also the black church leadership (Antioch Baptist and Trinity Methodist) that arranged for the purchase in 1872 of the land for Emancipation Park in the Third Ward so that black Houstonians could have a place for leisure activities after the city refused to provide such services for its black citizens.

The minister-leader exhibited a great deal of power and influence in the black community. The Houston Baptist Ministerial Alliance, for example, was an influential organization in the 1950s and 1960s. Rev. L. H. Simpson was probably the most influential local black minister-leader during this period.[4] Other influential black ministers have emerged over the years to continue this tradition. Among the more prominent black religious leaders in Houston in the mid-1980s were M. L. Price (Greater Zion Baptist Church), E. Stanley Branch (Fourth Missionary Baptist Church), Thomas Griffin (University Christian Church), M. M. Malone (St. John's Baptist Church), William ("Bill") Lawson (Wheeler Avenue Baptist Church), C. L. Jackson (Pleasant Grove Baptist Church), E. E. Coates (Wesley Chapel A. M. E. Church), F. N. Williams (An-

Rev. William ("Bill") Lawson, 1983 (photograph by Earlie Hudnall).

tioch Baptist Church, Acres Homes), Gene Moore (St. Agnes Missionary Baptist Church), and C. D. Daniels (Greater Jerusalem Baptist
Church).[5]

The sixties produced a number of black activist minister-leaders. For
example, Rev. William Lawson and Rev. Thomas Griffin led a number
of protest demonstrations in the mid-sixties against Houston's segregated public school system. They were also instrumental in the formation of an ad hoc group called PUSH (People for Upgraded Schools in
Houston). The group's main focus was to pressure the local school board
to speed up the desegregation of Houston's schools. The other three
members of PUSH were Francis Williams, E. M. Knight, and Barbara
Jordan.

The seventies and eighties saw a number of challenges to the traditional leadership structure that had its roots in the black church. This
trend held true in Houston and in the nation as a whole. Maulana Karenga contends that the black community has not been able to use the
church effectively since the civil rights movement.[6] Barnett and Vera
describe black leadership as being "inadequate and inappropriate for the
1980s": "the leadership is fragmented and often ineffective; policies are
phrased in civil rights terms and often based upon assumptions that
society will assist Afro-Americans' progress when the assistance may
be forthcoming, and the ultimate financial support for these leaders
comes from monied interests outside the Afro-American community."[7]

A number of sociological changes have contributed to the diversification of black leadership. For example, changing social and demographic
characteristics of the black population and the expanding education and
economic opportunity structure have broadened the black leadership
pool. The unmet needs and conditions—economic, psychological, and
physical—within the black community have also contributed to the empowerment of a new leadership.[8] New black leadership mechanisms are
needed to articulate and communicate the various public policy issues
that have an impact on the black community.[9]

The emergence of distinct leadership types (institutional, grass-
roots, and power elite) within Houston's black community signals a
maturation process within that group. The social, economic, and political gains made by black Houstonians in the seventies and eighties, along
with the in-migration of large numbers of blacks from outside the South
(many of whom were college educated) have no doubt altered the traditional framework and structure of black leadership in Houston. As in
most instances of change, the evolution of the current black leadership

structure did not come about without some degree of intragroup and ideological conflict. In the case of Houston, points of contention revolved largely around "natives vs. outsiders," "old guards vs. young bloods," "gatekeepers vs. activists," and "provincialism vs. universalism." Conflict in this case can be viewed as a healthy infusion of new ideas and varying ideologies.

A new black power elite leadership emerged in Houston during the late sixties and by the mid-seventies had in place the group of individuals who would challenge the city's resource allocation process (i.e., patronage jobs, city services, political power, etc.), which was overseen by the local power structure. For example, "The Group," an ad hoc assembly of black Houston leaders, was organized in 1975 by Larry Cager (who at the time was the director of the Houston Area Urban League). This leadership mechanism performed primarily a power-broker function between the black Houston community and Mayor Fred Hofheinz and the white power structure. The Group was better known among the downtown establishment than it was in the black areas such as Fifth Ward, Acres Homes, or Sunnyside.[10] The membership roster of this ad hoc lobbying group is presented in Table 10.1.

The eighties have seen numerous challenges to the black power-broker system and to the resource allocation process buttressed by the

Table 10.1. Membership Roster of "The Group," 1975.

Member	Occupational Background
J. Don Boney, Sr.	Educator
Larry Cager	Director, Houston Urban League
Art Higgs	Dentist
Mickey Leland	State representative
John B. Coleman	Physician/businessman
Judson Robinson, Jr.	City councilman
Anthony Hall	State representative
Otis King	Law school dean, TSU
Vince Rachal	Business executive
Al Hopkins	Pharmacist
Clarence Higgins	Businessman
A. M. Wickliff	Attorney
A. W. Parker	Labor leader
Granville Sawyer	President, TSU
Earl Lloyd	Physician
H. L. Garner	Labor leader (retired)
Rev. Bill Lawson	Minister
Judge Andrew Jefferson	District judge

Source: Harry Hurt III, "I Have a Scheme," *Texas Monthly* October, 1981, p. 248.

black power elite. The demise of The Group and its power elite orienta-
tion calls into question the efficacy of such a model in generating long-
term concessions for the larger black community.

The economic, psychological, and physical threats against black
people appear to have accelerated the convergence of once competing
forces within the black community. For example, recent black opposition to the racist white rule of the South African government has
brought numerous black organizations and their constituents closer together not only in their protests against apartheid, but in their assessment of the condition of the blacks in the United States. By taking this
worldview, black Houstonians are beginning to define their situation in
the broad context of other oppressed people of color. Moreover, this
ideological shift represents a giant step for black Houstonians, whose
world outlook had historically been confined to the "three T's": TSU,
Third Ward, and Texas.

CIVIL RIGHTS AND HOUSTON

Although Houston's black church leaders had established strong support
within the black community after emancipation, the beginning of the
twentieth century saw a small group of young black lawyers and businessmen join forces to challenge the second-class status of black Houstonians. By the early twenties, the city's black lawyers and businessmen
began to play a larger leadership role in black community affairs. For example, black lawyers such as Carter Wesley, Jack Atkins, James M. Na-
brit, Albert Dent, and John Murchison, and businessmen like Charles N.
Love (editor of the *Texas Freedman,* the first black newspaper in Houston), C. F. Richardson (editor of the *Informer* and first president of the
Texas Association of Branches of the NAACP), R. R. Grovey, L. L.
Spivey, and W. L. Dickerson combined forces and worked through the
local chapter of the NAACP to combat racial oppression and black political disenfranchisement.[11]

The black media and black editors played an important role in black
Houstonians' struggle for civil rights. The earliest challenges to the
whites-only Texas Democratic primary in the 1920s were in fact initiated by the black press. The importance of the black press was summarized in a 1967 report by the Harris County Council of Organizations:
"The Negro press in Houston has been another important organ of community protest, keeping before the Negro community the issues perti-

Above: Local protest against apartheid and South African Airways, 1983 (photograph by R. D. Bullard). *Below:* Julius and Lenora Carter, founders of the *Houston Forward Times* newspaper, 1970s (photograph courtesy of the *Houston Forward Times*).

nent to race relations in Houston. Thus, the Houston Negro press has been more than a business venture." [12]

The *Texas Freedman,* founded in 1893 by Charles Novell Love, was later published as the *Informer,* beginning in 1930. Carter W. Wesley, a well-known civil rights attorney, followed the example that had been set by his predecessors at the *Informer.* This tradition was continued in the 1960s by the *Forward Times,* a black newspaper founded by Julius Carter. The *Forward Times*'s photo essay section targeted controversial issues of the day, which included police misconduct, civil rights violations, and the political powerlessness of Houston's black community. Another black weekly, the *Houston Defender,* was established in 1930 by C. F. Richardson, Sr., and continues today under the same title.

The 1950s and 1960s also saw black Houstonians challenging segregation and the Jim Crow laws that controlled admission to the city's golf courses, libraries, public transportation, facilities in the new county courthouse, and the public school system. [13] Although many of the social problems that triggered large-scale protests, demonstrations, and urban riots of the sixties were present in Houston, the city's black community remained relatively calm during this period. However, the sixties did produce a series of sit-ins by black students at Texas Southern University. In the spring of 1960, for example, TSU students staged a lunch-counter sit-in at the nearby Weingarten store on Almeda Road in the Third Ward. Weingarten closed its lunch counter to keep from serving the TSU students. The sit-in protest by the students spread to Walgreens (located on Main at Elgin Street), and to the downtown area, where Woolworth's, Grant's, and the city hall's cafeterias were targets. Student demonstrations continued through the mid-sixties, with major disturbances occurring in 1965 and 1967.

Overall, the Houston black community as a whole was not mobilized during the sixties to the degree that many other black communities (e.g., Montgomery, Atlanta, Birmingham, Memphis, etc.) in the South were. This somewhat passive role of the black Houston community during the turbulent sixties can be traced to the changing leadership structure that was initially grounded in the black activist minister–businessman coalition. This coalition was well suited for frontal assaults on racial discrimination. However, the coalition was weakened somewhat in the early sixties with the push toward integration. Integration was especially threatening to black business owners; the goals were contradictory in that integration meant a potential loss of black clients to white businesses that only a short time before had refused to serve black

Houstonians. In a sense, Houston's black leaders and their organizations had become more conservative in the sixties than their counterparts in the thirties and forties.

CIVIL RIGHTS ORGANIZATIONS IN HOUSTON

Houston's civil rights and political organizations continue to play a role in blacks' struggle for parity. A listing of Houston's major civil rights and black political organizations is presented in Table 10.2. The NAACP is Houston's oldest civil rights organization, the Houston chapter having been founded in 1912. This black organization was the leading exponent of black political enfranchisement, school desegregation, and equal access to public facilities. A roster of the local organization's founding members includes Duke Crawford, Julius White, Rev. Miles Jordan, Newman Dudley, E. R. Nelson, Carter Wesley, Jack Atkins, C. F. Richardson, O. P. DeWalt, E. O. Smith, O. K. Manning, and Rev. J. S. Scott.

Lula B. White, wife of businessman Julius White, was probably the most prominent of the local NAACP leaders. She was the organization's executive secretary during the most active period (1942 to 1949) of the organization, the time that the NAACP was most prominent in the black community. The NAACP even survived an attempt in the early fifties by Texas Attorney General John Ben Shepperd to "run it out of the state." Membership in the local NAACP chapter peaked during the late 1950s,

Table 10.2. Houston Civil Rights and Political Organizations, 1984.

Organization	Year Founded
National Association for the Advancement of Colored People (NAACP)	1912
Houston Citizens Chamber of Commerce	1935
Houston Business and Professional Men's Club	1948
Harris County Council of Organizations	1949
Houston Lawyers Association	1953
Houston Area Urban League	1968
A. Phillip Randolph Institute	1968
Texas Black Political Caucus	1972
Black Organization for Leadership Development	1975
Houston Black United Front	1981
Progressive Action League	1982

with more than nine thousand members.[14] The shifting emphasis of the civil rights movement of the sixties, from litigation (the NAACP's primary strategy) to direct confrontation and civil disobedience, contributed to the diminished image of the NAACP and to the loss of membership and visibility of Houston's oldest black civil rights organization.

The local NAACP chapter was reorganized into eight branches (the Houston Metropolitan Council of Branches) in 1965 as a measure to regain lost membership and prestige in the black community. The membership under the new structure grew from 2,869 in 1965 to more than 3,500 in 1967. However, leadership and organization problems in the late sixties and seventies contributed to the decline of the NAACP's membership and prestige. The Houston NAACP, during this era, has been described as being "more successful in preventing civil rights militants from demonstrating than influencing white officials."[15]

The local branches of the NAACP were later restructured into a single chapter in 1980, and the organization is in a state of recovery from its earlier internal skirmishes. However, it is doubtful whether the local chapter will ever regain the prominence it had achieved during its early history. The membership of Houston's NAACP in February of 1985 was 2,185 (1,700 regular members and 485 life members).

The Harris County Council of Organizations is probably Houston's other most influential longstanding black civil rights and political organization. HCCO was founded on July 17, 1949. M. L. Ward, who at the time was president of the Greater Third Ward Civic Club, was installed as the organization's first president in a ceremony held at First Shiloh Baptist Church in the Third Ward.[16] The HCCO built its programs around voter registration, voter education, and "get-out-the-vote" activities, and the early years of the HCCO were concentrated on applying pressure to city officials (all of whom were white) to get municipal services—paved streets, libraries, police and fire protection, and so on—for the black community. The organization also focused its energies on police brutality within the black community and on local school desegregation. In a 1967 report of the HCCO, the problems, goals, and strategies of the black community are delineated: "The problems of poverty, neglect, and discrimination experienced by Houston's Negroes have constituted a significant impetus to an elaborate Negro organizational structure [HCCO]. The organizational programs inaugurated to effect change have included five main categories of strategies: citizenship education, litigation, protest and militancy, group work services, and welfare efforts."[17]

The HCCO, with its more than sixty black churches and civic organizations, has played a significant role in mobilizing black Houstonians in the civil rights and political arena. However, the organization has in recent years experienced a schism between its "old guard" and the "young bloods." For example, the HCCO went to court in the fall of 1981 to prohibit a faction of its young members from calling themselves the Harris County Council of Organizations Junior Council in political endorsements.[18] The HCCO Junior Council was led by a young Harvard-educated attorney, Sylvester Turner, and included some eighty other young black professionals. The HCCO Junior Council's endorsement of Al Green, a black candidate for mayor, was inconsistent with the endorsement by the parent organization of the incumbent, Jim McConn. The older faction of the HCCO prevailed in court, and the HCCO Junior Council was barred from using "HCCO" in its name. These events precipitated the birth of the Progressive Action League in 1982. The newly formed organization's membership roster largely comprised former HCCO Junior Council members.

Houston's other black civil rights and political organizations—Urban League, Black United Front, Black Organization for Leadership Development, and so on—served constituent groups within the larger black Houston community. While the goals and strategies of the city's local organizations may have differed in the past, this divergence has diminished in recent years. Many of Houston's black organizations now find themselves advocating not only traditional civil rights issues but also economic issues. Moreover, civil rights, economics, and politics are now viewed as inseparable elements in the black liberation movement. Because many of the problems faced by Houston's black community have not been eliminated (some have actually worsened), the need for these organizations will likely continue well into the twenty-first century.

There is little doubt that the work of the city's black civil rights and political organizations has paid off in terms of an expanded opportunity structure. For example, there were just a half-dozen black attorneys practicing law in Houston in 1953, the year Robert Hainsworth organized the Houston Lawyers Association, an all-black affiliation of local attorneys. The number of attorneys in the city grew to forty in 1967; in 1985 there were more than three hundred black attorneys in Houston.

An expanded opportunity structure has also meant more black participation in the operation of city government, where blacks had been systematically excluded. It was not until the 1950s that blacks were hired as firemen and policemen. The 1985 data from Houston's Affirmative Ac-

Table 10.3. Houston Municipal Work Force, January, 1985.

Employment Category	Ethnicity				Total
	White	Black	Hispanic	Other	
Administrators	603	224	96	36	959
	(63%)	(23%)	(10%)	(4%)	(100%)
Professionals	769	449	122	123	1,463
	(52%)	(31%)	(8%)	(9%)	(100%)
Technicians	726	438	126	56	1,346
	(54%)	(33%)	(9%)	(4%)	(100%)
Protective services[a]	181	195	64	5	445
	(40%)	(44%)	(15%)	(1%)	(100%)
Para-professional	14	32	9	1	56
	(25%)	(57%)	(16%)	(2%)	(100%)
Office/clerical	660	1,280	387	48	2,375
	(27%)	(54%)	(17%)	(2%)	(100%)
Skilled craft	646	778	365	64	1,853
	(34%)	(42%)	(20%)	(4%)	(100%)
Service/maintenance	382	2,739	603	188	3,912
	(9%)	(70%)	(16%)	(5%)	(100%)
Total	3,981	6,135	1,772	521	12,409
	(32%)	(50%)	(14%)	(4%)	(100%)

Source: Houston Affirmative Action Division, "City Workforce," January 1, 1985.
[a] Personnel from the fire and police departments are not included in the above totals.

tion Division show a total of 485 blacks in the city's fire department (15 percent) out of a total of 3,180 fire department personnel. Of the 3,912 city police personnel in 1985, 474 (11 percent) were black.[19]

The year 1964 marked the first time that blacks were hired for white-collar positions at city hall: Carolyn White was hired for a clerical position, and Huey Mitchell became the first black lawyer appointed to the city's legal department.[20] A distribution of the 1985 work force at Houston City Hall is presented in Table 10.3. Blacks made up one-half of the city's personnel in 1985. While blacks are found in all employment categories at city hall, they are concentrated in the office/clerical and service/maintenance positions. These two employment categories, which include mostly low-paying and low-skill jobs, account for one-third of the blacks who are employed by the city.

Black Houstonians have made significant inroads into the leadership positions within city government. Of the twenty-five city operations departments, five were headed by blacks in 1985 under Mayor Kathy Whitmire's administration: (1) Dr. James Haughton, Health Department; (2) Walter Jones, Human Resources Department; (3) Lee Brown, Police Department; (4) John Guess, Real Estate Department; and (5) Charles Ware, Solid Waste Management Department.

The appointment to city boards and commissions is another area where gains have been made since 1980. A total of fourteen blacks were appointed to city boards and commissions between 1980 and 1984. Despite these gains, blacks remain severely underrepresented on the city boards. Many of the city's more than fifty boards and commissions continue to be all white.

SCHOOL DESEGREGATION

Houston's educational institutions—elementary, secondary, and postsecondary—were traditionally segregated along racial lines, as was the case in most of the South. Educational facilities for blacks were often underfunded, neglected, and poorly staffed. Racial segregation in education (i.e., separate and unequal facilities) institutionalized advantages for whites at the expense of blacks.

Higher education for blacks in Houston began in 1927 with the creation of Houston Colored Junior College, which operated under Houston's school board. The junior college in 1934 was made a four-year institution and became Houston College for Negroes.[21] Houston College for Negroes operated from 1934 until 1947, when it became a state-supported institution and was renamed Texas State University for Negroes.

The creation of Texas State University for Negroes as a state-supported institution for blacks was a reaction to the threat of a lawsuit by the NAACP. In 1945 the NAACP was looking for a black plaintiff to challenge Texas' segregated university system. Heman Sweatt volunteered to serve as the test case for the NAACP, which targeted the University of Texas policy of excluding blacks from its law school.[22] Sweatt, a mail carrier and graduate of Wiley College in Marshall, was active in the local NAACP and in the National Alliance of Postal Workers; this group was at the time fighting discrimination against black postal workers. These activities reinforced Sweatt's ambition to become a lawyer.

While the team of NAACP lawyers was engaged in court litigation, the Texas legislature, in March, 1947, passed Senate Bill 140, which established a "Negro University" that would include a law school to be located in Houston. Thus, Texas State University for Negroes was created in an effort to keep Heman Sweatt out of the University of Texas law school and, in essence, was an extension of Jim Crowism. The school's name was changed in 1951 to Texas Southern University.

Heman Sweatt, whose lawsuit opened the way for blacks to enroll in graduate programs in Texas colleges and universities (photograph courtesy of the Houston Metropolitan Research Center, Houston Public Library).

Above: Texas Southern University, 1982 (photograph by Earlie Hudnall). *Below:* Thurgood Marshall School of Law at Texas Southern University, 1984 (photograph by Earlie Hudnall).

The U.S. Supreme Court resolved *Sweatt* v. *Painter* on June 5, 1950, when it ruled that Heman Sweatt must be admitted to the University of Texas law school. The Supreme Court ruling also compelled the University of Texas and similar state institutions to admit blacks to other graduate and professional schools. Two black students enrolled in University of Texas graduate programs in the summer of 1950: Horace Heath in a doctoral program in government and John Chase in the architecture program. Heman Sweatt enrolled in the University of Texas law school in the fall of 1950.[23]

The *Sweatt* v. *Painter* decision was an important precedent for the famous *Brown* v. *Board of Education* in 1954, which overturned the "separate but equal" doctrine, established by the high court's 1896 decision in *Plessy* v. *Ferguson*. It is somewhat ironic that Texas Southern University's law school is named in honor of Thurgood Marshall, the NAACP attorney who led the challenge to Jim Crow education. Despite the Thurgood Marshall School of Law's rather dubious beginning in 1947, it has produced more than two-thirds of the black lawyers practicing in Texas.

The desegregation of Houston's public schools began in 1956 (two years after the landmark U.S. Supreme Court decision of *Brown* v. *Board of Education*). The NAACP filed suit on behalf of two black girls, Beneva Williams and Delores Ross, to break up the city's dual education system. The Houston Independent School District (HISD) in 1960 was ordered by a federal court to begin a "grade-a-year" desegregation plan based upon "freedom of choice." The freedom-of-choice plan did little to desegregate the city's schools. The plan assumed that blacks would, given the choice, send their children away from ill-equipped black schools out to the well-endowed white schools. Black parents, however, were not that excited about sending their children into the hostile environment of white schools, and no one expected white parents to send their children to black neighborhood schools. In 1970, the federal courts ordered HISD to develop a new model for desegregation. The district submitted a modified plan in which the pairing of black and white schools was offered as a solution. This plan was later rejected by the courts because Hispanics, who at the time were counted as whites, were paired with blacks. The courts later ruled that Hispanics or "browns" had to be considered a separate racial/ethnic group. The district desegregation plan was again modified with primary emphasis placed upon the majority-minority transfer program and the "magnet school" concept.[24] The majority-minority transfer plan was set up to reduce the number of white students transferring outside the assigned school zone in an effort to skirt the desegregation plan.

The program requires the Houston Independent School District (HISD) to monitor transfers of students to determine the effect on integration. Students were encouraged to transfer from schools of one majority to another (white to black, brown to white, etc.), with free transportation provided by the schools. The magnet school concept is based on the idea that white parents will voluntarily enroll the children at inner-city schools offering specialized career programs and that black students would be attracted to such programs at schools in white areas. Magnet high schools in Houston include one for health professions, for engineering, and for the performing arts.

The HISD experienced a dramatic transition from a majority white district in the late sixties to a predominantly minority district in the eighties—a 62.8 percent decline in white pupil enrollment between 1968 and 1980. In 1970 the ethnic composition of the district was 49.9 percent white, 35.7 percent black, and 14.4 percent Hispanic.[25] By the fall of 1984, only 19.0 percent of the district's students were white, 43.6 percent were black, 34.2 were Hispanic, and 3.2 percent were of other races (see Table 10.4). On the other hand, the Houston area suburban school districts have largely white student populations (see Table 10.5).

Table 10.4. Enrollment in the Houston Independent School District by Race, 1970–84.

Year	Total Enrollment	Race of Students (in percent)			
		Black	Brown	White	Other
1970	241,138	35.7	14.4	49.9	—
1971	231,922	37.5	15.6	46.9	—
1972	225,397	39.4	16.6	44.0	—
1973	216,981	41.2	17.9	40.4	0.5
1974	211,574	41.9	19.0	38.6	0.5
1975	211,408	42.6	20.3	36.5	0.6
1976	210,025	43.1	21.8	34.2	0.9
1977	206,998	44.0	22.8	32.1	1.1
1978	201,960	45.0	24.2	29.4	1.4
1979	193,906	45.3	25.6	27.3	1.8
1980	194,043	44.9	27.8	25.1	2.2
1981	193,702	44.3	29.7	23.3	2.7
1982	194,439	44.1	30.9	21.7	3.3
1983	194,467	44.1	32.4	20.3	3.2
1984	187,031	43.6	34.2	19.0	3.2

Source: Houston Independent School District, "Pupil Enrollment Data 1970–1984," Pupil Enrollment Division, 1984.

Table 10.5. Ethnic Composition of Houston Area School Districts, 1980.

School District	Total Enrollment	Ethnic Composition of District (in percent)			
		White	Black	Hispanic	Other
Aldine	32,683	68.0	15.0	15.9	1.1
Alief	14,549	82.5	2.7	7.8	7.0
Channelview	4,366	90.0	1.0	9.0	0.0
Clear Creek	18,451	92.2	1.9	3.6	2.0
Crosby	2,451	55.0	43.0	2.0	0.0
Cypress-Fairbanks	20,233	86.9	4.2	5.7	3.1
Deer Park	8,211	91.4	0.2	7.9	0.5
Galena Park	11,648	74.0	8.0	18.0	0.0
Goose Creek	15,363	71.0	13.0	16.0	0.0
HOUSTON	**194,043**	**44.9**	**27.8**	**25.1**	**2.2**
Huffman	1,878	98.0	0.0	2.0	0.0
Humble	10,700	94.5	1.7	2.7	1.1
Katy	8,899	90.0	3.0	5.0	2.0
Klein	16,751	92.0	4.0	2.4	1.6
LaPorte	6,145	82.2	7.1	9.6	1.1
North Forest	17,731	14.8	85.2	0.0	0.0
Pasadena	36,483	74.8	1.7	20.9	2.6
Pearland	5,218	83.9	0.7	15.1	0.3
Sheldon	3,835	89.7	2.0	7.8	0.5
Spring	11,347	91.7	2.8	4.1	1.4
Spring Branch	34,611	86.1	2.9	6.8	4.2
Fort Bend	18,500	64.0	16.0	17.0	3.0
Tomball	2,980	91.0	6.0	2.0	1.0

Source: Texas Education Agency, "Pupil Enrollment Data," 1980.

The desegregation of Houston's public schools has been a long and controversy-filled struggle. Much of that controversy has centered around minority teacher hiring, teacher experience in poor and affluent schools, and the quality of educational programs in one-race minority schools. The Houston Area Urban League, in 1978, and black sociologist Kenneth Jackson, in 1983, observed that Houston's black and Hispanic schools have more teachers with less experience than do their white counterparts.[26]

A number of other factors have contributed to the increasingly political overtones of education administration in the district: teacher discontent, teacher assignment, teacher hiring and termination, school closings, pupil transfers, and the polarization of the school board along ideological and racial lines. The local school administration has often been accused of trying to guarantee employment of white teachers by manipulating the so-called Singleton Ratio, which refers to a 1970 U.S.

Fifth Court of Appeals decision in *Singleton* v. *Jackson Municipal Separate School District*. The court mandated that a specified black-to-white ratio be maintained in every school in the system. Moreover, the court required nondiscrimination in employment, demotions, and dismissals. The Singleton Ratio was thus designed to protect black faculty from wholesale dismissal following desegregation attempts. The Houston school board adopted the Singleton Ratio in February, 1970, calling for all HISD schools to have 65 percent white teachers and 35 percent black teachers; the ratio could have a variance of 5 percent. The hiring practices of HISD were challenged in 1983 by Barbara Mathews, a black science teacher. The lawsuit alleged that HISD engaged in old-fashioned racial discrimination when it turned down Mathews, who had more than four years of teaching experience, for a science position (an area where there is a national shortage of teachers) that was "reserved" for a white. Attorney Linda McKeever Bullard, who filed the case in U.S. District court, asserted that "hundreds of black college graduates are turned away while they're [HISD] recruiting whites for white-only positions." HISD in 1985 began recruiting teachers from as far away as Canada and Ireland to deal with its teacher shortage.[27]

The school district's hiring policies were called "insulting and racist" by some of its black teachers.[28] For example, faculty hiring breakdown within HISD in 1982 revealed that 673 teachers were hired in the summer. The racial composition of this group showed that 68 percent were white, 21 percent were black, and 11 percent were Hispanic. The district hired 242 new teachers in the summer of 1983. Of these newly hired teachers, 63 percent were white, 9 percent were black, and 28 percent were Hispanic.[29]

Houston's public schools were officially declared desegregated when Judge Robert O'Conor ruled in 1981 that HISD was a "unitary" system; this court ruling meant that the district had done everything possible to desegregate its schools (even though a substantial number of its schools remained "one-race" schools). After more than twenty-eight years, *Ross* v. *HISD*, the lawsuit that was filed by the NAACP against HISD, was finally settled out of court in the fall of 1984. A major point in the NAACP's argument had been equal access of minority students to the district's magnet school programs. While blacks made up more than 44 percent of the district's students, only 14 percent of the students enrolled in the district's magnet programs were black. The 1984 settlement agreement went to the heart of this matter, targeting district inner-city magnet schools' racial ratio at 60 percent minority and 40 percent white (from 50-50), and 65 percent minority and 35 percent white after July, 1985. The settlement also dealt with the issue of minority faculty recruitment.

The struggle for quality education will likely remain a key battleground because legislation, court orders, and settlements have not ended the disparate conditions under which many minority students are educated. There is continued concern that Houston's nonmagnet inner-city schools have become "invisible" or forgotten institutions because of the district's effort to stem "white flight."

BLACK POLITICAL EMPOWERMENT

There were more than 1.1 million blacks in Texas who were of voting age in 1980. However, only about 56 percent of this group was actually registered to vote. Moreover, only 41 percent of the black registered voters actually voted in the 1980 election.[30] Nearly two-thirds (61 percent) of the blacks in the Houston SMSA were registered to vote in 1980 and 49 percent actually voted in the November, 1980, election. Thus Houston's black community is a "sleeping giant" in political as well as economic terms. However, there is growing awareness of black potential in Houston and other major cities with large black populations. This awareness has intensified in recent years as a result of the Voting Rights Act of 1965, the nationwide voter registration program under Operation Big Vote, the broadening of the black leadership base with the growth of the black middle class, the increased visibility of the Congressional Black Caucus, and demographic trends which have made blacks the dominant ethnic bloc in many of the nation's cities.[31]

Black politics in Houston have come a long way since Dr. Lonnie E. Smith (a prominent black dentist) was refused a ballot in the 1940 all-white Harris County Democratic primary. The legal challenge of the white primary system culminated in the 1944 U.S. Supreme Court decision, *Smith* v. *Allwright,* which outlawed this practice.[32] However, not until fourteen years after *Smith* v. *Allwright* was the first black elected to a public office in Houston. Hattie Mae White (a former schoolteacher and the wife of a prominent black optometrist) was elected in 1958 to the HISD board; Asberry Butler was elected to the HISD board in 1964. One year after the passing of the Voting Rights Act of 1965, Barbara Jordan was elected to the Texas Senate and Curtis Graves was elected to the Texas House of Representatives. Judson Robinson, Jr. (whose father

Dr. Lonnie E. Smith, 1969 (photograph by Roy A. Smith).

Left: Hattie Mae White, first black elected to public office in Houston, 1962 (photograph courtesy of Hattie Mae White). *Right:* Judson Robinson, Jr., the first black elected to Houston City Council, 1980 (photograph courtesy of the Texas Southern University Archives).

was one of the city's pioneering black business entrepreneurs) in 1971 became the first black elected to the Houston City Council. The foundation for the election of these black officials was laid by such pioneering black community activists as Christin V. Adair, George Nelson, Moses and Erma LeRoy, Dr. Lonnie Smith, Fred Alston, Sid Hillard, John Butler, and other dedicated individuals who worked to make the black presence felt in the Harris County Democratic party.[33]

Some two decades after the passage of the Voting Rights Act, twenty-nine blacks hold elective office in Houston (see Table 10.6). Houston's blacks are represented at the city, county, state, and federal levels. The

Table 10.6. Black Elected Officials of Houston, January, 1985.

Elective Office or Government Body	Total All Houston Elected Officials	Number of Black Officials	Black Elected Officials
U.S. Congressman	6	1	George ("Mickey") Leland
State Senate	8	1	Craig Washington
State Representatives	26	5	Harold Dutton
			Al Edwards
			Larry Evans
			Sefronia Thompson
			Ron Wilson
Houston City Council	14	4	Rodney Ellis
			Anthony Hall
			Ernest McGowen, Sr.
			Judson Robinson, Jr.
Harris County Commissioners Court	5	1	El Franco Lee
Harris County Board of Education	7	1	Launey Roberts
State District Judge	48	3	Ken Hoyt
			John W. Peavy, Jr.
			Thomas H. Routt
Harris County Justice of the Peace	16	2	Betty Bell
			Alexander Green
Harris County Constable	8	1	A. B. Chambers
Houston Independent School District Board	9	3	Wiley Henry
			Herbert Melton
			Elizabeth Spates
North Forest Independent School District Board	7	7	Patricia Anderson
			Abner Brown
			Elwin Franklin
			Fran Gentry
			Edward King
			Maxine Seals
			Joe Stamps

period 1972–85 is significant in that Houston's black community elected the largest number of its members to public office in the city's history. The year 1985 saw a number of firsts: El Franco Lee (a former Texas legislator) became the first black elected to the five-member Harris County Commissioners Court, and Dr. Launey Roberts (a TSU education professor) became the first black elected to the seven-member Harris County Board of School Trustees.

Although Houston's black community made significant gains in the seventies and early eighties, the community's resources in recent years have been directed largely at electing black males to office. This pattern is not inconsistent with that of the larger white society, where resources are generally directed at electing white males.[34] This is not a small point when one considers the fact that the first black to be elected to a public office in the city was a woman (Hattie Mae White) and the first black to be elected to the Texas Senate was also a woman (Barbara Jordan). As of January, 1985, however, only six (or 20 percent) of the twenty-nine black elected officials in Houston were women.

The key to future black civil rights victories and effective black political empowerment is the presence of a well-organized, independent, and highly disciplined community structure. This organized political structure must work to elect not only black candidates but also candidates sympathetic to its interests, to develop a plan of action (an agenda), and to work with its candidates and other representatives to convert agenda items into workable public policy.[35] Conversely, the absence of economic muscle or clout mitigates the development of disciplined black political organizations that are not bashful about maximizing political power. Too often blacks have gone to great lengths to assure their adversaries that they do not wish to take over but merely to participate in the decision-making process.

Notes

CHAPTER I

1. John D. Kasarda, Michael D. Irvin, and Holly L. Hughes, "The South Is Still Rising," *American Demographics* 8 (June, 1986): 34.

2. For a thorough discussion of the rise of the South see Kirkpatrick Sale, *Power Shift: The Rise of the Southern Rim and Its Challenge to the Eastern Establishment* (New York: Random House, 1975); George Sternlieb and James W. Hughes, *Post-Industrial America: Metropolitan Decline and Inter-Regional Jobs Shift* (New Brunswick, N.J.: Rutgers University Center for Policy Research, 1975); David C. Perry and Alfred J. Watkins, eds., *The Rise of the Sunbelt Cities* (Beverly Hills, Calif.: Sage Publications, 1977); Franklin J. James, Betty I. McCummings, and Eileen A. Tynan, *Minorities in the Sunbelt* (New Brunswick, N.J.: Rutgers University Center for Policy Research, 1984).

3. U.S. Department of Housing and Urban Development (HUD), *Report of the President's Commission for a National Agenda for the Eighties* (Washington, D.C.: Government Printing Office, 1980), pp. 165–69; John D. Kasarda, "The Implication of Contemporary Trends for National Urban Policy," *Social Science Quarterly* 61 (December, 1980): 373–400; Richard M. Bernard and Bradley R. Rice, *Sunbelt Cities: Politics and Growth since World War II* (Austin: University of Texas Press, 1983), p. 15.

4. Perry and Watkins, *Rise of the Sunbelt Cities,* p. 277; Bernard and Rice, *Sunbelt Cities,* pp. 15–16.

5. James E. Blackwell, *The Black Community: Diversity and Unity,* 2nd ed. (New York: Harper and Row, 1985), p. xiii.

6. William C. Matney and Dwight L. Johnson, *America's Black Population: A Statistical View, 1970–1982* (Washington, D.C.: Government Printing Office, 1983), p. 1.

7. Ibid., pp. 1–2; Isaac Robinson, "Blacks Move Back to the South," *American Demographics* 8 (June, 1986): 40–43.

8. The U.S. Bureau of the Census divides the nation into four regions: South, Northeast, North Central, and West. The South Region includes the following seventeen states: Delaware, Maryland, District of Columbia, Virginia,

West Virginia, North Carolina, South Carolina, Georgia, Florida, Kentucky, Tennessee, Alabama, Mississippi, Arkansas, Louisiana, Oklahoma, and Texas.

9. See Gurney Breckenfeld, "Refilling the Metropolitan Doughnut," in Perry and Watkins, *Rise of the Sunbelt Cities,* p. 238.

10. Ibid., p. 239.

11. Chet Fuller, "I Hear Them Call It the New South," *Black Enterprise* 12 (November, 1981): 41.

12. Ibid., pp. 41-44.

13. See Robert D. Bullard, "Black Housing in the Golden Buckle of the Sunbelt," *Free Inquiry* 8 (November, 1980): 169-72.

14. U.S. Bureau of the Census, *State and Metropolitan Area Data Book 1982* (Washington, D.C.: Government Printing Office, 1982), p. 286.

15. See David G. McComb, *Houston: The Bayou City* (Austin: University of Texas Press, 1968); David G. McComb, *Houston: A History* (Austin: University of Texas Press, 1981); and Chandler Davidson, *Biracial Politics: Conflict and Coalition in the Metropolitan South* (Baton Rouge: Louisiana State University Press, 1972).

16. See R. D. Bullard, "Black Housing, Community and Economic Development," testimony presented to the U.S. Congress, House, Committee on the District of Columbia, *Problems in Urban Centers: Philadelphia, Los Angeles, Houston,* Hearing, 97th Cong., 1st and 2nd sess., June 15, 30, 1981 . . . February 12, 1982 (Washington, D.C.: Government Printing Office, 1983), pp. 382-404.

17. U.S. Bureau of the Census, *Advanced Estimates of Social, Economic, and Housing Characteristics: Texas* (Washington, D.C.: Government Printing Office, 1983), p. 145.

18. Ibid.

19. See Texas Employment Commission (TEC), "Houston District Labor Market Estimates: January, 1983, Affirmative Action Information" (Houston: Texas Employment Commission, 1983), p. 1 (mimeographed).

20. TEC, "Houston Regional Labor Market Estimates: January, 1986, Affirmative Action Information" (Houston: Texas Employment Commission, 1986), p. 1 (mimeographed).

21. Houston United Way, *Employment 1982: Report of the Priority Review Committee* (Houston: Houston United Way, 1982), pp. 26-27.

22. TEC, "Houston District Market Estimates," p. 3.

23. Karl E. Taeuber and Alma F. Taeuber, *Negroes in Cities: Residential Segregation and Neighborhood Change* (Chicago: Aldine Publishing, 1965), p. 41; Davidson, *Biracial Politics,* p. 133; Karl E. Taeuber, "Racial Residential Segregation, 28 Cities, 1970-1980," Center for Demography and Ecology Working Paper No. 83-12, (Madison: University of Wisconsin, 1983), p. 3 (mimeographed).

24. Breckenfeld, "Refilling the Metropolitan Doughnut," p. 239.

25. J. A. Kushner, *Apartheid in America: An Historical and Legal Analysis of Contemporary Racial Segregation in the United States* (Arlington, Va.: Carrollton Press, 1980), p. 130.

26. The Mayor's Urban Policy Advisory Board, *Toward an Urban Policy in Houston: A Report to the Mayor* (Houston: Mayor's Urban Policy Board, 1979), p. 84.

27. See William T. Wellman, *Portrait of White Racism* (Cambridge: The University Press, 1977); L. Knowles and K. Prewitt, *Institutional Racism in America* (Englewood Cliffs, N.J.: Prentice-Hall, 1970); Joe R. Feagin, *Discrimination American Style* (Englewood Cliffs, N.J.: Prentice-Hall, 1978); Stokley Carmichael and Charles V. Hamilton, *Black Power: The Politics of Liberation in America* (New York: Vintage Books, 1967).

28. For a thorough history of higher education for blacks in Houston see William E. Terry, *Origin and Development of Texas Southern University* (Houston: D. Armstrong, 1968), pp. 7–22.

CHAPTER 2

1. Kenneth Wheeler, *To Wear a City's Crown: The Beginning of Urban Growth in Texas, 1836–1865* (Cambridge, Mass.: Harvard University Press, 1968), p. 2.

2. O. F. Allen, *The City of Houston from Wilderness to Wonder* (Temple, Tex.: O. Fisher Allen, 1936), p. 1; Wheeler, *To Wear a City's Crown,* p. 109.

3. Don E. Carleton and Thomas H. Kreneck, *Houston Back Where We Started* (Houston: Houston City Magazine, 1979), p. 7.

4. See Henry A. Bullock, *Profile of Houston's Negro Business Enterprises: A Survey and Directory of Their Attitudes* (Houston: Negro Chamber of Commerce, 1962); and Henry A. Bullock, *Pathways to the Houston Negro Market* (Ann Arbor, Mich.: J. N. Edwards, 1957).

5. *Houston Defender,* June 18–24, 1982.

6. Economic Research Associates, *Fourth Ward Study: Phase A Reconnaissance* (Houston: City of Houston Economic Development Division Report, 1979), pp. 9–11.

7. National Urban Coalition, *Displacement: City Neighborhoods in Transition* (Washington, D.C.: National Urban Coalition, 1978), pp. 5–16.

8. Helen Sanders, "Antioch Baptist Church," *Black Focus,* December—January, 1977, pp. 6–8.

9. *Informer,* June 14, 1919.

10. McComb, *Houston: The Bayou City,* p. 157; Houston City Planning Department, *Report of the City Planning Commission* (Houston: City of Houston, 1929), p. 25.

11. Houston Community Development Division, "Survey of the Riceville Area of Activity," December 3, 1980, p. 3. This windshield survey was conducted for the specific purpose of documenting the physical conditions of the neighborhood for inclusion in the city's Community Development Block Grant Program.

12. Anna Sonier and L. Rice, longtime residents of Riceville community, interviews with the author, June, 1983; *Houston Chronicle,* June 18, 1978.

13. Ginger A. Hester, "Bordersville: Catching Up to the 20th Century," *Playsure Magazine,* January, 1980, p. 20.

14. *Houston Post,* December 13, 1981.

15. Houston City Planning Department, *Houston: Year 2000* (Houston: City of Houston, 1980), p. II-3.

16. U.S. Bureau of the Census, *Data Book 1982*, p. 386.
17. Bullock, *Pathways to the Houston Negro Market*, pp. 60–61.
18. Ibid., pp. 61–62.
19. Houston City Planning Department, *Houston Analysis: Low, Moderate Income Areas* (Houston: City of Houston, 1978), p. 113.
20. Bullock, *Pathways to the Houston Negro Market*, p. 61.
21. Houston City Planning Department, *Near Northside Fifth Ward Community Development Data Book* (Houston: City of Houston, 1979).
22. R. D. Bullard and D. L. Tryman, "Strategies in Neighborhood Redevelopment: A Case Study of Houston's Fifth Ward," paper presented at the meeting of the Southwestern Sociological Association, Dallas, Tex., March 25–28, 1981, p. 4.
23. See Demographic Environs Research, *Economic Development Strategies for Revitalizing Houston's Fifth Ward* (Houston: City of Houston Economic Development Division, 1980).
24. See R. West, "Only the Strong Survive," *Texas Monthly*, February, 1979, pp. 94–105; Houston Economic Development Division, *City of Houston Overall Economic Development Program for the Economic Development Target Area* (Houston: City of Houston, 1978).
25. Alfred Calloway, president of the Houston Citizens Chamber of Commerce, interview with the author, March, 1982.
26. See R. D. Bullard, *Houston's Third Ward: A Center of Black Business* (Houston: Texas Southern University, 1982); Carolyn Jenkins, "Business and Economic Development in the Black Community: Houston's Third Ward," master's thesis, Texas Southern University, 1982.

CHAPTER 3

1. U.S. Bureau of the Census, *America's Black Population 1970 to 1982: A Statistical Review* (Washington, D.C.: Government Printing Office, 1983), pp. 20–23; U.S. Bureau of the Census, *The Social and Economic Status of the Black Population in the United States: An Historical View, 1790–1978* (Washington, D.C.: Government Printing Office, 1979), p. 136.
2. HUD, *The President's National Urban Policy Report: 1980* (Washington, D.C.: Government Printing Office, 1980), p. 523.
3. U.S. Bureau of the Census, *Annual Housing Survey Current Housing Reports*, Series H-150-77 (Washington, D.C.: Government Printing Office, 1977); Houston City Planning Department, *Houston: Year 2000*, p. 24.
4. HUD, *A New Partnership to Conserve America's Communities: A National Urban Policy* (Washington, D.C.: Government Printing Office, 1978); HUD, *Annual Housing Survey: 1979 Current Housing Report* (Washington, D.C.: Government Printing Office, 1981).
5. See Robert W. Lake, "Racial Transition and Black Home Ownership in American Suburbs," *Annals of the American Academy of Political and Social Sciences* 441 (January, 1979): 142–56; F. D. Wilson, *Residential Consumption, Economic Opportunity, and Race* (New York: Academic Press, 1979), pp. 74–

75; R. D. Bullard, "Persistent Barriers in Housing of Black Americans," *Journal of Applied Social Sciences* 7 (Fall–Winter, 1983): 19–31.

6. Lake, "Racial Transition and Black Home Ownership," pp. 142–56; Phillip Clay, "The Process of Black Suburbanization," *Urban Affairs Quarterly* 14 (June, 1979): 405–23; Kathryn P. Nelson, *Recent Suburbanization of Blacks: How Much, Who, and Where?* (Washington, D.C.: HUD, 1979), p. 26; R. D. Bullard, "The Black Family: Housing Alternatives in the 80's," *Journal of Black Studies* 14 (March, 1984): 341–51.

7. Nelson, *Recent Suburbanization of Blacks*, p. 5.

8. Bullock, *Pathways to the Houston Negro Market*, pp. 62–64.

9. Mayor's Urban Policy Advisory Board, *Toward an Urban Policy in Houston* (Houston: City of Houston, 1979), p. 84.

10. Bullock, *Pathways to the Houston Negro Market*, p. 64.

11. Larry Long and Donald Dahlman, *The City-Suburbs Income Gap: Is It Being Narrowed by a Back-to-the-City Movement?* (Washington, D.C.: Government Printing Office, 1980), p. 20; R. P. Nathan, "New Crisis Downtown," *Society* 16 (1979): 5–8.

12. See National Urban Coalition, *Displacement*, p. 13; Phillip L. Clay, *Neighborhood Renewal* (Lexington, Mass.: Lexington Books, 1979), chap. 2; S. B. Laska and D. Spain, eds., *Back-to-the-City* (New York: Pergamon Press, 1979); Elizabeth Ashton, "Nearer to Town Than Thee," *Houston City Magazine* 3 (1979): 43–48; Bullard, "The Black Family," pp. 341–51.

CHAPTER 4

1. See Housing Authority of the City of Houston, *First Annual Report*, July 1940. This 32-page report illustrated the slum conditions in the city and in the drawings of projects planned for the city. At the time, more than 25,680 families (or more than 87,618 individuals) were living in substandard dwelling units that were scattered across the city.

2. Houston City Planning Department, *Houston: Year 2000*, p. v–18; Housing Authority of the City of Houston, *Annual Report of the Housing Authority of the City of Houston*, July, 1984, p. 3.

3. Under the city's Housing Assistance Payments Program, eligible low- and moderate-income households pay approximately one-fourth of their income for housing; Houston's housing authority pays the remainder of the tenants' rent. This subsidy program is funded under Section 8 of the Housing and Community Development Act of 1974 and is administered through the U.S. Department of Housing and Urban Development.

4. Houston Community Development Office, "Community Development Program Application," 1979 (mimeographed).

5. See the *Houston Post*, February 11, 1940; Housing Authority of the City of Houston, *Allen Parkway Village/Fourth Ward Technical Report* (Houston: Housing Authority of the City of Houston, 1983), p. II-7.

6. See R. D. Bullard and O. L. Pierce, "Black Housing Patterns in a Southern Metropolis: Competition for Housing in a Shrinking Market," *Black Scholar* 11 (November–December, 1979): 65.

7. Charles Taylor, director of planning and development for the Housing Authority of the City of Houston, interview with the author, September 12, 1984.

8. See Economic Research Associates, *Houston's Fourth Ward Study;* also Housing Authority of the City of Houston, *Allen Parkway Village,* chap. 5.

9. Housing Authority of the City of Houston, *HACH Occupancy Report,* Housing Management Division, August 31, 1984.

10. R. D. Bullard, "Does Section 8 Promote an Ethnic and Economic Mix?" *Journal of Housing* 35 (July, 1978): 364–65. This article was part of a larger study of Houston's Housing Assistance Payments Program (i.e., Section 8 program).

CHAPTER 5

1. See W. Hellmuth, "Homeowner Preference," in *Comprehensive Income Taxation,* ed. J. A. Pechman (Washington, D.C.: Brookings Institution, 1977).

2. HUD, *A New Partnership to Conserve America's Communities: A National Urban Policy* (Washington, D.C.: Government Printing Office, 1978), p. 69.

3. U.S. Commission on Civil Rights, *The Federal Fair Housing Enforcement Efforts* (Washington, D.C.: Government Printing Office, 1979), p. 6.

4. Ibid., p. 230.

5. See J. Saltman, "Housing Discrimination: Policy Research, Methods, Results," *Annals of the American Academy of Political and Social Sciences* 441 (January, 1979): 186–96.

6. See HUD, *How Well Are We Housed: Blacks* (Washington, D.C.: Government Printing Office, 1979); HUD, *The President's National Urban Policy Report: 1980* (Washington, D.C.: Government Printing Office, 1980).

7. See J. F. Kain, *National Urban Policy Paper on the Impact of Housing Discrimination and Segregation on the Welfare of Minorities,* policy paper prepared for HUD, Office of Community Planning and Development (Cambridge, Mass.: Harvard University, 1980); F. D. Wilson, *Residential Consumption, Economic Opportunity, and Race* (New York: Academic Press, 1979); R. D. Bullard and D. L. Tryman, "Competition for Decent Housing: A Focus on Complaint Activity in a Sunbelt City," *Journal of Ethnic Studies* 7 (Winter, 1980): 51–63; R. D. Bullard, "Persistent Barriers in Housing Black Americans," *Journal of Applied Social Sciences* 7 (Fall–Winter, 1983): 19–32.

8. J. Newitt, "The Future of Home Sweet Home," *American Demographics* 2 (November–December, 1980): 17–19; R. D. Bullard, "The Black Family: Housing Alternatives in the 80's," *Journal of Black Studies* 14 (March, 1984): 341–51.

9. R. W. Marans, M. Colton, R. Graves, and B. Thomas, *Measuring Restrictive Rental Practices Affecting Families with Children: A National Survey* (Washington, D.C.: HUD, 1980), p. 71.

10. J. G. Green and G. P. Blake, *How Restrictive Rental Practices Affect Families with Children* (Washington, D.C.: Government Printing Office, 1980), p. 34.

11. See Richard Muth, *Cities and Housing* (Chicago: University of Chicago Press, 1969); A. Sorensen, K. E. Taeuber, and L. J. Hollingsworth, Jr., "Indexes of Racial Residential Segregation for 109 Cities in the United States, 1940–1970," *Sociological Focus* 8 (1975): 125–42; T. L. Van Valey, W. C. Roof, and J. E. Wilcox, "Trends in Residential Segregation, 1960–1970," *American Journal of Sociology* 82 (1977): 826–44.

12. G. E. Simpson and M. Yinger, *Racial and Cultural Minorities: An Analysis of Prejudice and Discrimination* (New York: Harper and Row, 1972); John Yinger, "A Model of Discrimination by Landlords," Institute for Research on Poverty Discussion Paper 251-75 (Madison: University of Wisconsin, 1975).

13. John Kain, "Housing Market Discrimination, Home Ownership and Savings Behavior," *American Economic Review* 62 (June, 1972): 263–77.

14. Wilson, *Residential Consumption, Economic Opportunity, and Race*, p. 108.

15. HUD, *The President's National Urban Policy Report* (Washington, D.C.: Government Printing Office, 1978), pp. 68–69.

16. See Chester Hartman, *Housing and Social Policy* (Englewood Cliffs, N.J.: Prentice-Hall, 1975); Michael N. Danielson, *The Politics of Exclusion* (New York: Columbia University Press, 1976).

17. Jim McConn, mayor of Houston, presenting his views on fair housing, in City of Houston, *Houston, A City of Neighbors: 1977 Fair Housing Division Annual Report* (Houston: Fair Housing Division, 1977), p. 1.

18. City of Houston, *Houston Fair Housing Division Annual Report* (Houston: Fair Housing Division, 1976), p. 1.

19. The Houston city attorney receives those housing discrimination complaints which the Fair Housing Division evaluates as having sufficient evidence to prosecute. However, only one housing discrimination case has reached the court stage in the history of the city's Fair Housing Ordinance; this case was subsequently dismissed.

20. R. D. Bullard and D. L. Tryman, "Competition for Decent Housing," pp. 51–63.

21. The ethnic composition of the one hundred randomly sampled housing discrimination complaints included fifty-seven blacks, twenty-three whites, sixteen Hispanics, and four Orientals.

CHAPTER 6

1. Robert L. Lineberry, *Equality and Urban Policy: The Distribution of Municipal Public Services* (Beverly Hills, Calif.: Sage Publications, 1977), p. 11.

2. David M. Smith, "Who Gets What, Where and How: A Welfare Focus for Human Geography," *Geography* 59 (November, 1974): 294.

3. F. H. Buttel and W. L. Flinn, "Social Class and Mass Environmental Beliefs: A Reconsideration," *Environment and Behavior* 10 (September, 1978): 433–50; Barbara Blum, *Cities: An Environmental Wilderness* (Washington, D.C.: Environmental Protection Agency, 1978), p. 3.

4. Daniel Zwerdling, "Poverty and Pollution," *The Perspective* 37 (January, 1973): 26.

5. Ibid.; R. D. Bullard and Beverly H. Wright, "The Politics of Pollution: Implications for the Black Community," *Phylon* 47 (March, 1986): 71–78.

6. See S. Deutsch and D. Van Houten, "Environmental Sociology and the American Working Class," *Humboldt Journal of Social Relations* 2 (Fall–Winter, 1974): 22–26; D. E. Morrison, "The Environmental Movement: Conflict Dynamics," *Journal of Voluntary Action Research* 2 (Spring, 1973): 78–85; L. Tucker, "The Environmentally Concerned Citizen: Some Correlates," *Environment and Behavior* 10 (September, 1978): 389–418; A. Schnaiberg, *The Environment: From Surplus to Scarcity* (New York: Oxford University Press, 1980), pp. 362–411.

7. Zwerdling, "Poverty and Pollution," p. 27; Bullard and Wright, "The Politics of Pollution," p. 72.

8. Robert P. Burden, "The Forgotten Environment," in *The Effects of Man-made Environments on Health and Behavior,* ed. Lawrence E. Hinkle and William C. Loring (Washington, D.C.: Government Printing Office, 1977), p. 49.

9. Susan C. Cutter, "Community Concern: Social and Environmental Influence," *Environment and Behavior* 13 (January, 1981): 105–24.

10. See J. N. Smith, *Environmental Quality and Social Justice in America* (Washington, D.C.: The Conservation Foundation, 1974).

11. Constance Perrin, *Everything in Its Place: Social Order and Land Use in America* (Princeton, N.J.: Princeton University Press, 1977).

12. Ann B. Shlay and Peter Rossi, "Keeping Up the Neighborhood: Estimating the Effect of Zoning," *American Sociological Review* 46 (December, 1981): 705.

13. See Harvey Molotch, "The City as a Growth Machine: Toward a Political Economy of Place," *American Journal of Sociology* 82 (1976): 309–32; John R. Logan, "Growth, Politics and the Stratification of Places," *American Journal of Sociology* 84 (1978): 404–16; Shlay and Rossi, "Keeping Up the Neighborhood," pp. 703–19.

14. *Houston Post,* February 1, 1948; *Business Week,* January 14, 1948, p. 48.

15. *Houston Post,* December 18, 1959, June 19, 1961, January 2–10, 1962.

16. McComb, *Houston: A History* pp. 158–59.

17. *Houston Chronicle,* April 29, 1979.

18. *Houston Post,* July 6, 1980.

19. *Houston Post,* March 3, 1983.

20. The Houston City Council adopted the drafting of the comprehensive plan without ever using the word "zoning." For a more thorough account of the events surrounding the council's actions see *Houston Post,* September 13, 17, 1986; *Houston Chronicle,* September 14, 1986.

21. The Houston Environmental Survey 83 was part of a larger quality-of-life study in the Department of Sociology at Texas Southern University in the spring of 1983.

22. Quoted in *Houston Chronicle,* May 30, 1983.

23. Cutter, "Community Concerns," p. 105.

24. D. Wahl and R. L. Bancroft, "Solid Waste Management Today: Bringing About Municipal Change," *Nation Cities* 13 (August, 1975): 18–32.

25. See Bullard, "Does Section 8 Promote an Ethnic and Economic Mix?" pp. 364–65; Bullard and Tryman, "Competition for Decent Housing," pp. 51–63; R. D. Bullard, "Endangered Environs: The Price of Unplanned Growth in Boomtown Houston," *California Sociologist* 7 (Summer, 1984): 84–102.

26. S. P. Hays, "The Structure of Environmental Politics since World War II," *Journal of Social History* 14 (Summer, 1981): 719–38.

27. Michael H. Brown, *Laying Waste: The Poisoning of America by Toxic Chemicals* (New York: Pantheon Books, 1980), p. 267; John C. Fine, "A Crisis of Contamination," *Sciences* (March–April, 1984): 20–24.

28. Congressional Office of Technology Assessment, *Technologies and Management Strategies for Hazardous Waste Control* (Washington, D.C.: Government Printing Office, 1983), p. 3.

29. Brown, *Laying Waste*, p. 99.

30. The case study of Houston's municipal solid waste disposal system was developed from in-depth interviews in 1982 with personnel from Houston's Solid Waste Management Department and the Houston Air Quality Control Board. Initial contacts were made by telephone with both city departments, and personal interviews were undertaken with key administrative personnel. Field notes were taken during these interviews. On-site visits were made to the disposal facilities to verify the data obtained from the interviews.

31. See R. D. Bullard, "Solid Waste Sites and the Black Houston Community," *Sociological Inquiry* 53 (Spring, 1983): 273–88; Bullard, "Endangered Environs," pp. 85–101; R. D. Bullard and B. H. Wright, "Endangered Environs: Dumping Grounds in a Sunbelt City," *Urban Resources* 2 (Winter, 1985): 37–39; Bullard and Wright, "The Politics of Pollution," pp. 71–78; S. Pollack, J. Grozuczak, and P. Taylor, *Reagan, Toxics and Minorities* (Washington, D.C.: Urban Environment Conference, 1984); Urban Environment Conference, Inc., *Taking Back Our Health: An Institute on Surviving the Toxic Threat to the Minority Community* (Washington, D.C.: Urban Environment Conference, 1985).

32. See Bullard, "Solid Waste Sites," pp. 279–81; Bullard, "Endangered Environs," pp. 93–97.

33. Texas Department of Health, *Municipal Solid Waste Regulations* (Austin: Texas Department of Health, 1977), p. 16.

34. For a detailed account of this dispute see *Houston Chronicle*, November 8, 11, 15, 22, 1979, December 15, 22, 1979, June 19, 1980; *Houston Post*, December 15, 1981.

35. *Houston Chronicle*, June 19, 1980.

CHAPTER 7

1. Houston Chamber of Commerce, *Houston Facts 81: Current Facts Concerning the Nation's Fifth Largest City* (Houston: Houston Chamber of Commerce, 1981).

2. U.S. Department of Labor, "City Workers, Family Budgets," Labor Statistics, Autumn, 1977.

3. U.S. Department of Labor, "Autumn, 1982 Urban Family Budgets," Autumn, 1981.

4. TEC, *Job Scene 1985, Employment Projection by Specific Industries and Occupations* (Houston: Texas Employment Commission, 1977).

5. Ibid., pp. 1–5.

6. TEC, "Houston District Labor Market Estimates: December, 1981, Affirmative Action Information" (Houston: Texas Employment Commission, 1981).

7. TEC, "Houston District Labor Market Estimates," January, 1983.

8. See Robert Hill, *The Widening Economic Gap* (Washington, D.C.: National Urban League, 1979); National Urban Coalition, *The Situation in Urban America: A Spring 1982 Report* (Washington, D.C.: National Urban Coalition, 1982); National Urban League, *The Status of Black America* (Washington, D.C.: National Urban League, 1983).

9. Matney and Johnson, *America's Black Population,* p. 4.

10. U.S. Bureau of the Census, *Advanced Estimates of Social, Economic, and Housing Characteristics* (Washington, D.C.: Government Printing Office, 1983), p. 145; Matney and Johnson, *America's Black Population,* p. 9.

11. Houston Job Training Partnership Council, *Annual Report Program for 1985* (Houston: HJPTC, 1985), p. 23.

12. U.S. Bureau of the Census, "Population Profile of the United States, 1981," *Current Population Reports,* Series P-20, No. 374, 1982, table 6-3.

13. Matney and Johnson, *America's Black Population,* pp. 16–17.

14. John Reid, "Black America in the 1980s," *Population Bulletin* 37, no. 4 (December, 1982): 23.

15. U.S. Bureau of the Census, *Advanced Estimates of Social, Economic, and Housing Characteristics,* p. 145.

CHAPTER 8

1. Minority Business Development Agency, *Minority Business Enterprises Today: Problems and Their Causes* (Washington, D.C.: U.S. Department of Commerce, 1982), p. 1.

2. Ibid., p. 7.

3. See David Caplovitz, *The Merchants of Harlem* (Beverly Hills, Calif.: Sage Publications, 1973); also Samuel I. Doctors and Ann S. Huff, *Minority Enterprises and the President's Council* (Washington, D.C.: Ballinger Publishing, 1973).

4. See James E. Blackwell, *The Black Community: Diversity and Unity* (New York: Gold, Mead, and Co., 1974), pp. 219–42; also Roy F. Lee, *The Setting for Black Business Development* (Ithaca, N.Y.: Cornell University Press, 1972).

5. Robert E. Nelson, "Education and Entrepreneurial Initiatives," in *Small Enterprise Development: Policies and Programmes,* ed. Phillip A. Neck (Geneva: International Labor Office, 1979).

6. Small Business Administration Task Force, *Report of the SBA Task Force on Venture and Equity Capital for Small Business* (Washington, D.C.: Small Business Administration, 1977).

7. See Timothy M. Bates, *Black Capitalism: A Quantitative Analysis* (New York: Praeger Publications, 1973); Irvin Light, *Ethnic Enterprise in America* (Berkeley: University of California Press, 1972).

8. See U.S. Bureau of the Census, *1977 Survey of Minority Business Enterprises: Blacks* (Washington, D.C.: U.S. Government Printing Office, 1979).

9. E. R. Bourdon, J. D. Fisk, D. M. Fisk, O. E. Roth, and K. R. Winch, "Economic Prospects for Blacks in the 1980's," report from the Congressional Research Service, December, 1981, p. 34.

10. Andrew Brimmer, "Blacks in Business in the 1980's: More Salaried Managers than Owners," *Black Enterprise* 12 (July, 1982): 30.

11. Sue Marshall and D. H. Swinton, "Federal Government Policy in Black Community Revitalization," *Review of Black Political Economy* 10 (Fall, 1979): 25.

12. Earl G. Graves, "On Top of Black Businesses," *Black Enterprise* 11 (June, 1981): 15.

13. Robert S. Browne, "Institution Building for Urban Revitalization," *Review of Black Political Economy* 10 (Fall, 1979): 38.

14. See U.S. Bureau of the Census, *Provisional Estimates of Social, Economic, and Housing Characteristics* (Washington, D.C.: Government Printing Office, 1981).

15. Cleveland A. Chandler, "The Size and Shape of the Black Economy," *Crisis* 89 (March, 1982): 10; Andrew Brimmer, "Trends and Prospects for Black Business," *Black Enterprise* 16 (July, 1986): 29.

16. Chandler, "Size and Shape," pp. 10-11.

17. Bourdon et al., "Economic Prospects for Blacks in the 1980's," p. 32.

18. See David Birch and Susan MacCracken, *Corporate Evolution: A Microbased Analysis* (Washington, D.C.: Small Business Administration, 1981).

19. U.S. Bureau of the Census, *1982 Survey of Minority-owned Business Enterprises: Blacks* (Washington, D.C.: Government Printing Office, 1982), p. 87.

20. Ibid., table 7.

21. "Top 100 Black Businesses," *Black Enterprise* 11 (June, 1981): 121-29.

22. Ibid., 13 (June, 1983): 109-10.

23. Ibid., pp. 125-26.

24. Mack H. Hannah has been called the "dean of black business entrepreneurs" in Texas and for years was considered the "richest black man in Texas." In addition to starting Standard Savings and Loan Association, he founded Hannah Life Insurance Company, Hannah Funeral Home, and Gulf Western Mortgage Company. He has also been an active real estate developer in Houston and in the Texas Gulf Coast region.

25. "Savings and Loans," *Black Enterprise* 13 (June, 1983): 125-26.

26. See *Houston Chronicle*, September 4, 1984.

27. See John C. Davenport, "Call Me Frenchy: Taking Creole to the Masses," *Houston City Magazine*, September, 1984, p. 162.

28. Jenkins, "Business and Economic Development in the Black Community," p. 69.

29. Ibid., pp. 70-72.

30. See R. D. Bullard, *Black Houston Business Survey* (Houston: Texas Southern University Publication, 1983).

31. Blackwell, *The Black Community,* pp. 237–38.

CHAPTER 9

1. Houston Police Department, *Assessment of the Department Problems and Issues* (Houston: Houston Police Department, 1982), p. 1.

2. See Herman Goldstein, *Policing a Free Society* (Cambridge, Mass.: Ballinger Publishing, 1977); William J. Bopp, *Police Community Relationships* (Springfield, Ill.: Charles C. Thomas, 1972).

3. David Jacobs, "Inequality and Police Strength: Conflict Theory and Coercive Control in Metropolitan Areas," *American Sociological Review* 44 (December, 1979): 913–25.

4. Louis A. Radelet, *The Police and the Community* (Encino, Calif.: Glenco Press, 1977), chap. 1.

5. Lee P. Brown, "Bridges over Troubled Waters: A Perspective on Policing in the Black Community," in *Black Perspectives on Crime and the Criminal Justice System,* ed. Robert L. Woodson (Boston: G. K. Hall and Co., 1977), pp. 86–87.

6. Jacobs, "Inequality and Police Strength," p. 922.

7. Brown, "Bridges over Troubled Waters," p. 94.

8. See K. L. Sindwani and R. D. Bullard, *Police Roles in the Inner-City* (Houston: Texas Southern University Report Series, 1977).

9. George Napper, "Perceptions of Crime: Problems and Implications," *Black Perspectives on Crime and the Criminal Justice System,* ed. Woodson, p. 5.

10. Houston Police Department, *Assessment of the Department Problems and Issues,* pp. 14–17.

11. Mayor's Urban Policy Advisory Board, *Toward an Urban Policy in Houston,* p. 84.

12. Houston Police Department, *Assessment of the Department Problems and Issues,* p. 1.

13. Blackwell, *The Black Community,* 2nd ed., p. 256.

14. Ibid., pp. 256–57.

15. *Houston Chronicle,* August 2, 1981.

16. Milton D. Morris, *The Politics of Black America* (New York: Harper and Row, 1975), pp. 231–34; Abraham S. Blumberg and Arthur Niederhoffer, *The Ambivalent Force: Perspectives on the Police* (New York: Holt, Rinehart and Winston, 1985), pp. 411–12.

17. Houston Police Department, "Community-oriented Policing Program Grant Application," May 13, 1983, p. 5.

18. Ibid., pp. 5–6.

19. Ibid., pp. 10–11.

20. Blackwell, *The Black Community,* pp. 260–61.

21. Brown, "Bridges over Troubled Waters," p. 85.

22. Ibid., p. 88.

23. Chandler Davidson, *Biracial Politics: Conflict and Coalition in the Metropolitan South* (Baton Rouge: Louisiana State University Press, 1982), p. 121.

24. Houston Police Department, *Assessment of the Department Problems and Issues,* p. 51.

25. Henry A. Bullock, *The Houston Negro Murder Problem: Its Nature, Apparent Causes and Probable Cures,* Report of the Mayor's Negro Law Enforcement Committee (Houston, 1961), p. 80.

26. *Houston Press,* April 15, 1931.

27. Edgar Schuler, "The Houston Negro Riot," *Journal of Negro Education* 29 (1944): 300.

28. Ibid., pp. 321–22.

29. Robert V. Haynes, *A Night of Violence: The Houston Riot of 1917* (Baton Rouge: Louisiana State University Press, 1976), pp. 167–69.

30. John Hope Franklin, *From Slavery to Freedom: A History of Negro Americans* (New York: Alfred A. Knopf, 1974), p. 340.

31. Ibid., pp. 340–41.

32. Haynes, *A Night of Violence,* pp. 322–23.

33. National Advisory Commission on Civil Disorders, *Report of the National Advisory Commission on Civil Disorders* (New York: E. P. Dutton and Co., 1968), p. 41.

34. Ibid., pp. 40–41.

35. Davidson, *Biracial Politics,* pp. 84–85; *Forward Times,* May 27, 1967; Bill Helmer, "Nightmare in Houston," *Texas Observer,* June, 1967.

36. Davidson, *Biracial Politics,* p. 84.

37. Brown, "Bridges over Troubled Water," p. 83.

38. R. D. Bullard, *Fear of Crime, Fear of Police and Black Residents' Endorsement of Crime-reduction Strategies* (Houston: Texas Southern University Report Series, 1981).

CHAPTER 10

1. See Robert B. Hill, "The Economic Status of Black America," in *The State of Black America 1981,* ed. James D. Williams (New York: National Urban League, 1981), pp. 1–51; Charles V. Willie, *Class and Caste Controversy* (Bayside, N.Y.: General Hall, 1979); Charles V. Willie, *Race, Ethnicity and Socioeconomic Status: A Theoretical Analysis of Their Relationship* (Bayside, N.Y.: General Hall, 1983).

2. Maulana Karenga, "The Crisis of Black Middle-class Leadership: A Critical Analysis," *Black Scholar,* (Fall, 1982): 31; Daniel C. Thompson, *The Negro Leadership Class* (Englewood Cliffs, N.J.: Prentice-Hall, 1963), pp. 5–6.

3. Dennis E. Poplin, *Communities: A Survey of Theories and Methods of Research* (New York: Macmillan, 1979), pp. 215–18.

4. Harris County Council of Organizations, *Profile of the Negro Community* (Houston: Harris County Council of Organizations, 1967), pp. 39–43.

5. Lovenger H. Bowder, "Black Family, Black Church," *Black Experience* 4 (December, 1981): 20–23.

6. Karenga, "The Crisis of Black Middle-class Leadership," p. 28.

7. Marguerite Ross Barnett and Ndoro Vincent Vera, "Afro-American Politics and Public Policy Priorities in the 1980s," *Black Scholar* 11 (March–April, 1980): 9–21.

8. King E. Davis, "The Status of Black Leadership: Implications for Followers in the 1980s," *Journal of Applied Behavioral Science* 18 (1982): 309–22.

9. Milton D. Morris, *The Politics of Black America* (New York: Harper and Row, 1975), p. 285.

10. Harry Hurt III, "I Have a Scheme," 9 *Texas Monthly* (October, 1981): 248–49.

11. Ira B. Bryant, *Texas Southern University: Its Antecedents, Political Origin and Future* (Houston: Ira B. Bryant, 1975), p. 27.

12. Harris County Council of Organization, *Profile of the Houston Negro Community*, p. 35.

13. McComb, *Houston: A History*, p. 166.

14. Davidson, *Biracial Politics*, p. 29; Harris County Council of Organizations, *Profile of the Houston Negro Community*, pp. 33–34.

15. Davidson, *Biracial Politics*, pp. 30–33.

16. Harris County Council of Organizations, *Profile of the Houston Negro Community*, p. 3.

17. Ibid., p. 33.

18. *Houston Post*, October 24, 1981.

19. Data obtained from Lee Elliot Brown, director of Houston's Affirmative Action Division, "Fire and Police Departments," January 1, 1985, pp. 1–2.

20. McComb, *Houston: A History*, p. 171; Harris County Council of Organizations, *Profile of the Houston Negro Community*, p. 29.

21. William E. Terry, *Origin and Development of Texas Southern University* (Houston: D. Armstrong, 1968), pp. 16–27.

22. See Michael L. Gillette, "Heman Marion Sweatt: Civil Rights Plaintiff," in *Black Leaders: Texans for Their Times*, ed. Alwyn Barr and Robert A. Calvert (Austin: Texas State Historical Association, 1981), pp. 157–90.

23. Ibid., p. 181.

24. Houston Area Urban League, *Quality Education and Minority Educational Opportunity* (Houston: Houston Area Urban League, 1978), pp. 1–2.

25. Gary Orfield, *School Desegregation Patterns in the States, Large Cities and Metropolitan Areas 1968–1980* (Washington, D.C.: Joint Center for Political Studies), p. 31.

26. Houston Area Urban League, *Quality Education and Minority Educational Opportunity*, pp. 33–35; Kenneth Jackson, "Toward Quality Education: The Case of HISD" (Houston: Texas Southern University Report Series, June, 1983), p. 23.

27. *Houston Chronicle*, October 21, 1983; *Houston Post*, May 23, 1985.

28. *Houston Chronicle*, September 16, 1983.

29. *Houston Post*, September 8, 1983; *Houston Chronicle*, September 16, 1983.

30. U.S. Bureau of the Census, *Voting and Registration in the Election of November 1980*, Series P-20, No. 370 (Washington, D.C.: U.S. Government Printing Office, 1982), pp. 31–34.

31. Thomas E. Cavanaugh, "The Reagan Referendum: The Black Vote in the 1982 Election" paper presented at the annual meeting of the Midwest Political Science Association, Chicago, Ill., April 20–23, 1983, pp. 1–2.

32. Donald S. Strong, "The Rise of Negro Voting in Texas," *American Political Science Review* 42 (1948): 513.

33. Harris County Council of Organizations, *Profile of the Houston Negro Community*, pp. 41–43.

34. Albert K. Karnig and Susan Welsh, *Black Representation and Urban Policy* (Chicago: University of Chicago Press, 1980), p. 472.

35. Mack H. Jones, "Black Political Empowerment in Atlanta: Myths and Reality," *Annals of the American Academy of Political and Social Sciences* 439 (September, 1978): 90–117.

Index

Invisible Houston was composed into type on a Mergenthaler Linotron 202 digital phototypesetter in ten point Times Roman with two points of spacing between the lines. Times Roman was also selected for display. The book was designed by Jim Billingsley, composed by G&S Typesetters, Inc., printed offset by Thomson-Shore, Inc., and bound by John H. Dekker & Sons. The paper on which the book is printed bears acid-free characteristics for an effective life of at least three hundred years.

TEXAS A&M UNIVERSITY PRESS : COLLEGE STATION

CPSIA information can be obtained
at www.ICGtesting.com
Printed in the USA
BVHW082013020222
627630BV00003B/355